ESCAPE
FROM THE
BLACK HOLE

The true story of a former hip-hop artist.

internet movies televi
dvds video games concer
rpgs d&a chat gems name
instant messaging email
pornography music comics
magazines peer pressure
pop culture fan clubs

ebm punk
industrial
rap techno hip-hop
pop fusion reggae
alternative new age rock
deep house jazz blues
swing dance trance
rave disco country
soul acid organic

I V O R   M Y E R S

Pacific Press® Publishing Association
Nampa, Idaho
Oshawa, Ontario, Canada
www.pacificpress.com

Cover design by Mark Bond
Cover design resources from iStockphoto.com
Inside design by Steve Lanto

Copyright © 2007 by
Pacific Press® Publishing Association
Printed in the United States of America
All rights reserved

Unless otherwise indicated, all Scripture quotations are from the
King James Version of the Bible.

Scriptures quoted from NIV are from THE HOLY BIBLE, NEW
INTERNATIONAL VERSION, copyright © 1973, 1978, 1984
International Bible Society. Used by permission of Zondervan Bible
Publishers.

Additional copies of this book are available from two locations:
3ABN: Call 1-800-752-3226 or visit http://www.3abn.org
Adventist Book Centers: Call 1-800-765-6855
or visit http://www.adventistbookcenter.com

3ABN Books is dedicated to bringing you the best in published
materials consistent with the mission of Three Angels Broadcasting
Network. Our goal is to uplift Jesus through books and audio and
video materials by our family of 3ABN presenters. Our in-depth
Bible study guides, devotionals, biographies, and lifestyle materials
promote the whole person in health and the mending of broken
people. For more information, call 616-627-4651 or visit 3ABN's
Web site: http://www.3abn.org

ISBN 13: 978-0-8163-2198-8
ISBN 10: 0-8163-2198-1

Author's Web site: http://www.poweroflamb.com

07 08 09 10 11 · 5 4 3 2 1

CONTENTS

DEDICATION

To my mother, whose influence and consistent revelation of love for her children had much to do with shaping my character.

Sean, thank you for allowing God to lead you in the making of this true life story. A special thanks to Benjamin Baker and Gordon Kainer for your help with this manuscript. I am grateful to my church family for believing in me, in Christ, and for giving me the opportunity to bring you the Word of God. Danny, thank you for standing behind us. Ralph, I will always remember lunch! And to my wife Atonte, who has been everything to me and has stood by my side in good times and hard times—I love you.

Ivor Myers, the privileged husband of Atonte Myers

INTRODUCTION

And there was war in heaven: Michael and his angels fought against the dragon; and the dragon fought and his angels, and prevailed not; neither was their place found any more in heaven. And the great dragon was cast out, that old serpent, called the Devil, and Satan, which deceiveth the whole world: he was cast out into the earth, and his angels were cast out with him.
—Revelation 12:7–9

We were called The Boogie Monsters, a hip-hop artist group signed to EMI Records. My younger brother, Sean, and I took our stage names from the characters in the fictional blockbuster movie trilogy Star Wars. I called myself Yoda, after the 900-year-old Jedi Master known for his wisdom and his mastery of "the Force." I fit the role of my assumed persona well. I was the one in search of hidden wisdom. Malcolm X had been one of my heroes from my youth, and I had always wanted to copy him—if not in doctrine then at least in spirit. People even said that I looked like him! I fed my mental and spiritual energies on whatever I could glean from Islam, New Age, ancient Egyptology, or even *Star Wars*. After all, the hip-hop culture is not without its "spiritual" dimension. Sean was known as Jedi, after the Jedi warriors who were called to settle conflicts around the galaxy.

As rappers, we considered ourselves intellectuals, warring against evil in a secular setting, and after years of paying our dues, we finally made it to stardom. We would come to believe that we could war against the evils of this world through our music, but, imperceptibly, God would reveal to us the real "Star War"—a war that was far from fiction and beyond our wildest imaginations. This war eventually would cause us to give up all that we once held important and bring us together with the invisible forces of good under the leadership of the God of the universe.

The Bible specifically speaks of a major "star war" in the book of Revelation. A long time ago, in a galaxy far, far away "there was war in heaven: Michael and his angels fought against the dragon; and the dragon fought and his angels, and prevailed not; neither was their place found any more in heaven. And the great dragon was cast out, that old serpent, called the Devil, and Satan, which deceiveth the whole world: he was cast out into the earth, and his angels were cast out with him" (Revelation 12:7–9).

This galactic battle began in heaven and spilled out across the universe to a battlefield called earth. Lucifer, the highest of all angels, sought to usurp God's throne (see Isaiah 14:12–14; Ezekiel 28:13–18). Through his cunning deception he recruited one-third of the angels in heaven! "And his tail drew the third part of the stars of heaven, and did cast them to the earth" (Revelation 12:4). Satan has carried on this rebellion for more than six thousand years, but the final conflict is about to take place.

In the Bible, stars represent angels, both good and bad (see Job 38:7; Revelation 12:4, 9). They also can represent God's people (see Daniel 12:3), as well as rebellious people (see Jude 13). Throughout Scripture these stars are divided into two sides—dark and light, and they're constantly at war.

The conflict is real. The stakes are eternal. The ultimate "Star" in this war is Jesus Christ. In the Old Testament, Balaam prophesied of Christ when he said, "I shall behold him, but not nigh: there shall come a Star out of Jacob, and a Sceptre shall rise out of Israel" (Numbers 24:17).

John the revelator recorded the words of Christ: "I Jesus have sent mine angel to testify unto you these things in the churches. I am the root and the offspring of David, and the bright and morning star" (Revelation 22:16).

In this war, the purpose of the fallen stars is to draw humanity's attention away from the Bright and Morning Star, Jesus Christ. One of the most effective ways in which they have succeeded is by using the human "stars" of the entertainment industry. What terror I felt when I realized that I had been an unwitting agent of the dark side—a star compelling people to worship and idolize human beings instead of the One who created them!

But God called me to leave the forces of evil and the powers of the dark side. He called me to link up with the forces of good and the Prince of Light.

Little did I realize in those days that the *Star Wars* series was nothing more than a counterfeit of the heavenly star war, in which the destiny of millions would be decided. In this conflict people are influenced by stars of good or evil, becoming either stars for God, turning many to righteousness, or stars against Him, exalting themselves above their fellow humans and above God.

The Lord began to speak to me through His Word about the entertainment industry—what I call "the black hole," "the dark empire," or "the dark side." Some have said that nothing can escape the powerful pull of a black hole, but I'm here to testify that there is an even greater power—the healing, saving, transforming power of God's grace.

This is the story of my conversion from the dark side to the light, my escape from the black hole!

The Boogie Monsters—Yoda (Ivor Myers), Jedi, (Sean Myers), Vex, (Sean Pollard), and Mondo (Mondo McCann). 1995.

Ivor shares his testimony for the first time before thousands at Soquel camp meeting in California. 1999.

1

THE MAKING OF A DARK-SIDE WARRIOR

I was born in Kingston, Jamaica, in 1972, the third of four sons. I grew up in a home where respect was the most important principle, and although we rarely attended any church, our parents taught us to have respect for our elders and other people. They were strict disciplinarians, and the belt often was used to help cure any problems we kids were having.

Our family was close knit; I always thought of my two older brothers, Tony and Rhoan, as my bodyguards. In turn, the three of us were bodyguards for my younger brother, Sean.

And Dad was the *family* bodyguard.

Born in Saint Thomas, Jamaica, Dad came from a broken family, the second of six siblings. His mother left for England when he was only twelve, leaving him to be raised by his grandparents. His grandfather, a Church of God minister, brought him up in that religion. Dad put himself through school, graduating at the top of his class, and then he began working as a civil servant and a reserve officer. In the reserves he became the commander of a platoon of forty men. He went on to join the Jamaican Special Forces, where he led clandestine operations, internal security, and reconnaissance missions. Finally he became part of the military covert counterintelligence unit, where he was an instructor in martial arts. With this background, he never would allow his sons to lose a fight.

My mother was born in the parish of Hanover, Jamaica; as a child she attended the Holiness Church of God. When she was only four years old, her father left to make a home for her and her mom in England. He told his wife-to-be (my grandmother) he'd send for her once he had settled there, but he fell in love with another woman he met while en route to England and married her instead. My mother did not see her father again until she was an adult. In spite of this, she had a happy childhood. Her experiences growing up with her four siblings and a large extended family explain why she emphasized the importance of the family to us boys.

Although both my parents had attended church when they were young, they had both wandered away from religion by the time I was born. However my father was encouraged by a Catholic bishop and friend to have me christened as a baby. Sean, eleven months younger, was christened as well.

Our childhood in Jamaica was peaceful until the event that would separate us from our parents for more than six months. In Jamaica, the military was often at war with drug lords, and my father led many of the raids. Moved by unseen dark-angel warriors, one group of drug dealers plotted revenge. One weekend my father was away, leaving us children and mom at home. Night had settled when Rhoan, then twelve, headed for the door to play. It was then that the reflection of something shiny in the moonlight caught his eye from one of windows in the house. Turning to investigate, he noticed two men on either side of the window, masked and holding guns. In an instant he was running and yelling to Mom.

At the same time, our next-door neighbor also saw what was happening, grabbed his gun, and began shooting in the air to scare off the intruders. None of us knew enough about angels at the time to credit our protection to them, but they were surely present that day!

After this incident, my parents decided that for the safety of our family we must leave the country; they set their eyes on America. Leaving us in the care of close military friends, Mom and Dad left to find work and set up a new home for us. The events that came next were to shape my future years as a teenager and young adult in sad and sinister ways.

While in the care of these close family friends, Sean and I were also taken care of by a hired baby sitter who turned out to be a student of the dark side. Daily she molested my brother and me, and over time the abuse created an early appetite for sexual behavior. At the tender age of five, I was already being trained under Satan, being made into a dark-side warrior by the emperor of the dark empire. I became sexually active with young girls while most other kids my age had no inkling of what sex was all about. This behavior followed me through my teenage and young adult years. At the time I thought this was cool. The more women I had been with, the more important I felt. I didn't realize that this was, and continued to be, one of Satan's most effective methods of destroying one's desire for a single mate for life, leading to the destruction of so many marriages today.

Those months in Jamaica without Mom and Dad were confusing and sad. Sean and I couldn't understand why they had deserted us. We had no idea they were doing what they thought was best for us. But as painful as it was for us, I now realize that the separation was even more painful for them! And, of course, they were totally unaware of the abuse we were suffering in their absence.

They would send us letters and toys. They even called, but nothing could take the place of *being* with them. When they finally sent for us, I was excited and angry at the same time. In fact, my little mind plotted revenge! The whole plane ride from Jamaica to New York, I was seething with six-year-old wrath. When we arrived at LaGuardia International Airport, I remained calm so as not to give myself away. Spotting our parents, we took off running, Sean for Mom, and I for Dad. As he scooped me up in his arms, that's when I let him have it, right in the chest! My little five-year-old fists meant business.

"Why did you leave me?" I cried out. My father was taken aback for a moment. Then he laughed and held me even tighter—a hug that in an instant melted away all the sadness of the previous six months. The results of the abuse, however, would leave a scar that lasted much longer.

The year was 1978, and the place was Brooklyn, New York. The sights and sounds of the city captivated us. *This is all so different from Jamaica,* I thought. I had never seen so many lights, high-rise buildings, and stores. The intriguing taste of pizza tickled my tongue for the first time, and I remember my first bowl of corn flakes. The city seemed to never sleep! Even the air felt different. I curiously studied my new surroundings and quickly noticed that even the accents of the people differed from mine. We were mesmerized with America! But this would also be the place where we would come face-to-face with a black hole that would nearly destroy our souls.

2
INTRODUCTION TO THE EMPIRE

Among the ghettos of New York, a dark force was beginning to move into a new phase. It went by the name "rock 'n' roll." Its roots came from the music of the early part of the century, but during the '50s and '60s it brought millions of young people under its rebellious power. Through it, the spirit of rebellion against God had become popular and cool. When our family arrived in New York, this musical force of rebellion against God was taking on a new guise—it was called hip-hop.

It began in the 1970s in the Bronx and quickly became popular among Blacks and Hispanics. Becoming a culture in itself, three main elements made it popular: *Emceeing* is the art of putting words that rhyme to syncopated music, with the drum or percussion beat that is basic to rock, jazz, and rhythm and blues. This idea came primarily from my home country, Jamaica. The second element of hip-hop is *d-jaying*, a form of blending different styles of music, again with syncopation as its main ingredient. Finally, there is the art of *break dancing*. This colorful, acrobatic, and warlike dance style was adapted from a Brazilian martial art called *Capoeira,* "The Dance of War," which was developed in the 1500s by slaves revolting against their masters in that country. The word *capoeira* means an area of the forest or jungle that has been cleared by burning or cutting down trees. Slaves would practice this art to music as a way of training or "battling" one another in a clearing or a circle. Marked by deft, tricky movements, often played on the ground or inverted, it has a strong acrobatic component, using groundwork, sweeps, kicks, and other aggressive movements.

From a social standpoint, hip-hop was viewed as a way of supposedly reducing gang violence. Many angry, rebellious kids channeled their aggression into the art, making it their vehicle of expression. Police officers often confused these dance "battles" on the street corners for gang fights.

Sean and I were captivated by break dancing, graffiti, and hip-hop music. As we watched the kids around us, listened to their strange slang phrases, noticed their styles of dress, and saw the popularity of this emerging culture, we wanted to be a part of it all.

It was difficult for many of my fellow first-graders to understand me when I spoke, because of my Jamaican accent. Whenever I opened my mouth, I was laughed at or mocked; so, naturally, my self-esteem was very low. My school teachers didn't provide much help. I vividly remember my first-grade teacher, a middle-aged Caucasian man, stopping at my desk one morning. He smiled at me; I smiled back. "A face only a mother could love," he declared, still smiling.

I thought he was telling me how much my mother loved me, and I continued smiling as he walked away. Later that day, I asked Mom what that phrase meant—"a face only a mother could love." I didn't tell her why I was asking.

When she told me, the teacher's words wounded my self-confidence deeply.

I soon began refusing to speak in class, even when addressed by the teacher. I developed a fear of public speaking that continued for many years. But no words were needed to break dance; it was a quick way of making new friends and gaining acceptance from my peers.

Nonetheless, I still had a difficult time fitting in with other kids and would often end up in fights. I wasn't a bully, but I refused to be pushed around. I also had a very strong sense of justice! When I was in the third grade, I saw a bigger student fighting a smaller one. I jumped into the fight to defend the smaller kid, shouting, "Fight for justice! Fight for justice!"

In second grade I met Tamarat—T for short. T and I instantly became friends. We both had active imaginations. Watching *Star Wars* for the first time, I was thinking, *What would it be like to be Luke Skywalker?* I imagined being in a controversy of universal proportions and being able to travel around the universe between galaxies. We often would daydream heroic scenarios of life-and-death situations requiring sacrifice, honor, and sometimes even the heart-wrenching, but heroic, death of the central figure! Anytime we came up with a new scenario, we'd begin by saying, "Imagine this . . ." And after our scenario had been carefully painted on the canvas of our imaginations, we would yell out in excitement and awe. No wonder other kids thought we were weird!

T, Sean, and I got involved in martial arts at an early age. Sean had been born on the opening night of Bruce Lee's film *Enter the Dragon*. Mom, who was watching the film, had to leave the drive-in movie theater to deliver Sean, but she came back a few nights later to finish the movie. So, Sean came by his love of martial arts honestly. He was a kung-fu junkie! He got to the point that he refused to eat without chopsticks!

As kids, we were introduced to Shaw Brother's films. Every Saturday at 3:00 P.M., the Fox station in New York would air a different Chinese-produced kung-fu movie with poorly dubbed English. This soon became a sacred time for Sean and me. We began to study the martial arts, in particular Wing Chun. We also got involved with Ninjitsu, a Japanese martial art based on stealth. It was used by ninjas, who were often assassins and masters of blending into their surroundings whether snow, forests, or the night. We also were intrigued with the philosophies underlying the various martial-arts systems. The dragon, emblem of the martial arts, became our favorite symbol. We especially loved to go to some backwoods area to practice with the sword and many other weapons. By the time we got to junior high school we were becoming very good at it.

Junior high school was like a jungle. Kids had their lunch money taken on a regular basis. Large "crews," sometimes as many as twenty kids, terrorized other students who had few friends. Infamous names such as Linky, Marcello, Todd R., and LaMarco struck fear in the hearts of students at our junior high school. My friends and I resorted to the martial arts for protection. Six of us formed The Ninja Alliance. We collected a formidable arsenal of weaponry, including the *manriki-kusari* (a chain with iron weights on either side), *nunchakus* (a pair of hardwood sticks joined by a chain), swords, blowguns, smoke bombs, Chinese throwing stars and darts, grappling hooks, hand-and-foot claws, staffs, fans, and much more.

On a daily basis, T, Sean, and I would come up with elaborate imaginary scenarios of being in class, when some alien attackers would rise out of the floor, sending the other kids into a hysterical panic. In the midst of the pandemonium, I would "radio" T and Sean, who were already aware of the situation because the same thing was happening in their classrooms! It would now be up to us to ward off the forces of evil using our martial arts and our superpowers. At times it seemed we were doomed, but we always managed to come out the victors, saving the day, after winning our peers' admiration, who would never look at us the same again! These imaginary exploits were a mental rush for us!

Later the martial arts really would become our protection. Sean gained respect because of his gymnastic ability and his quick feet. Once, while he and a friend were play fighting, he suddenly stopped while being chased, jumped in the air, and with a reversed roundhouse kick, took off a friend's glasses!

Sometimes the martial arts would get me in trouble because it made me unafraid to face anyone. A kid named Rob had been bullying me for some time. One day the teacher stepped out of the classroom. Rob walked up to me and punched me on the arm. Now, since Rob had many friends and I had so few, I didn't want to have a run-in with him.

"Stop!" I said. He replied with another punch, this time harder.

"Stop!" I said again. He did it a third and fourth time. I snapped. Picking up a chisel (it was a shop class), I chased Rob around the room. *He was running from me!* I had just gotten within reach of my tormenter when the teacher came back into the classroom and stopped the fight. I expected to get jumped by at least twenty kids after school, but, surprisingly, Rob never bothered me again.

My brother and I also were fascinated by the entertainment industry—what I now call "the force." Every day we would play Batman and Robin. *Superman*, the movie with Christopher Reeves, mesmerized us. Michael Jackson's "Beat It" and "Thriller" made him an idol to many of us. At the same time, New Edition, a group of young boys singing about young love, had come on the scene. It was the first time we realized that kids could be famous too.

We were intrigued with Béla Lugosi's *Dracula*, Lon Chaney's *The Wolf Man*, and Boris Karloff in *Frankenstein*. Our dad didn't allow us to read or watch such material, but Sean especially persisted until one day Dad found out and gave him a memorable spanking. It's probably not coincidental that years later our music group would become known as The Boogie Monsters.

The best day of the week for us was Saturday. Television cartoons ran like a marathon from 7:00 A.M. until noon. A few hours later, the Saturday afternoon kung-fu movies followed! Saturday was our glued-to-the-TV-screen day!

Other groups like KRS-One, Run-D.M.C., UTFO, and movies like *Beat Street,* portraying life in the ghettos, made the lifestyle of hip-hop more and more appealing. We were indeed bombarded by the force of the entertainment industry.

Meanwhile, the vice that Satan had introduced me to as a child continued to grow stronger. At age twelve, I already had experienced the fear of possibly becoming a father, along with wondering if I had contracted HIV or some other sexually transmitted disease. Thoughts of an early death plagued me, and I often wondered what would happen to me if I died.

Was there a God who could save me from these fears? I questioned why I would have to die and wondered who would take care of me and watch over me in that dark place called death. I remember sitting in the backseat of our car when I was six years old, watching an old man walking by. I leaned forward, keeping my eyes on him.

"Mommy, do we all have to die?" I asked.

Perhaps sensing my fear or not having an answer herself to the mysteries of death, she replied, "Not if you don't want to."

I was relieved, but the dreams and thoughts of death persisted. Hearing rumors of a place called hell added to my anguish, but I didn't share these feelings with anyone. It was my own private nightmare.

Living in an empire where the only light is a glittering promise of temporary fame, money, and pleasure—an empire where everything leads only to death—was depressing, even for a young mind like mine. How I wished I could escape from this world into one of my own creation! I knew the worlds I created in my imagination weren't reality, but what I didn't know was that there was another reality besides the world I lived in. A reality that far surpassed anything I could imagine in my most vivid dreams. Unknown to me, God's reality waited for me to discover it.

I received my first Bible for my seventh birthday—the first one I celebrated in America. I was fascinated with it. Even though our family did not go to church, I distinctly remember the sense of awe that came over me—an almost holy feeling. I felt that this Book would empower me to do something mighty. But my life went on pretty much as it had, and it wasn't long before I had forgotten this special feeling.

Though I now had a Bible, my first introduction to the book of Revelation came through a movie I watched when I was twelve years old. *The Omen* is the story of a young boy named Damien who discovers that he is the antichrist. In the movie, his guardian demon tells him to read Revelation 13, and he learns about the mysterious number 666. After searching under his hair, Damien makes the shocking discovery that the number 666 is on his forehead! From then on, anyone who finds out his identity is mysteriously killed.

This movie terrified me, since it was the first time I had heard about something called the "mark of the beast." Shortly after this, we met Susan, our fourteen-year-old cousin from England. She had come to spend the summer with us, and we took an instant liking to her. She was friendly, had an interest in God, and would often talk to us about the Bible.

One day Susan, Sean, and I were home alone, when Susan began to talk to us about Bible prophecy and the number 666.

"You know that number *really is* in the Bible," she said in a low tone.

"Plus," she continued, "there are companies that work for the devil. They produce dishwashing liquids and laundry detergents, and the way you can tell they work for the devil is to look at the boxes and bottles their soap comes in. You'll find the sign of the beast on them!"

"What's the sign of the beast?" I asked, immediately wishing I hadn't.

"Well," Susan replied, "it's a picture of a half-moon with a man's face in it."

My brother and I were trembling.

"Do you have some detergent in the house?" she asked. I wondered if she was trying to scare us to death.

"Yes. It's downstairs in the laundry room."

"Then let's go!" she commanded.

I didn't want to go. According to the movie, whoever found out Damien's true identity died a mysterious and horrible death! But pulled along unwillingly by a strange curiosity, we followed Susan down the steps to the laundry room. It looked to me at this point like a dark dungeon. Finding the box of soap, Susan began to inspect it closely. She peered at the front of the box then turned it and inspected the back. Finally she slowly scanned the side panel.

Our hearts were pounding.

"There it is! There it is!" she whispered. I could hear horror music playing in the background. Then I saw it! *The half-moon with a man's face in it.* We were so terrified we ran screaming out of the house in our pajamas!

My concept of God and the devil left me feeling trapped between two torturers with no way of escape. But this would begin to change one night in 1985.

It was Halloween night, a holy day for the dark side. I was thirteen, and Sean, my friends, and I were getting ready to go trick-or-treating as we had done every year. We were on our bicycles, riding around town, when suddenly my father drove up. We were surprised he found us, but we were even more surprised when he said, "You're not going trick-or-treating!"

Sean and I were stunned. What had we done to deserve this?

"Why?" we asked as respectfully as we could. His answer stunned us even more.

"Because Halloween is the devil's holiday!"

We had never heard our father even seriously mention the devil before, but now we found ourselves in the backseat of the car, heading to my aunt Carmen's Pentecostal church. There we were to spend Halloween in a church, watching a movie about Jesus!

That night, a star war had been fought for my father's mind. The Holy Spirit had victoriously moved my dad to come find his children and bring them to church. As I sat there, a war was raging over my own young soul too. Dark warriors, angry at losing the battle for my father's mind, pressed the spirit of anger upon me for being snatched away from my Halloween expedition. I sat there, seething, as holy warriors carried out the divine mission to open my mind just a little!

After some time my anger and confusion subsided, and I became interested in this Man whose name I had heard used only in jest or in swearing. As I sat watching the movie about Jesus, I could feel a spirit of calmness coming over me. I didn't know that this was a taste of His Spirit of peace, offered to every soul who comes to Jesus (see Matthew 11:28). After the movie, I thought, *I wouldn't mind learning more about Jesus.* But the thought left me as quickly as it had come.

Then one day shortly after this our uncle began to talk to us about something he had been studying. It had to do with the Bible, and he had come to the conclusion that the Sabbath was on Saturday, not on Sunday. This blew my mind. One definite thing I *knew* about Christianity was that Sunday was the day that everyone went to church.

I asked Uncle Tony what he was going to do about his newfound knowledge, and he replied, "I'm going to have to start keeping the Sabbath on Saturday, now that I know about it!" The thought stirred in my mind for some time, but then it was gone.

These events ignited in me a desire to learn about prophecy and what lay in the future, but the appeal of various Black Power movements, popular with the rappers of the day, eclipsed these desires. The Nation of Islam, for example, and the Five Percenters were spreading anti-Bible sentiments through music. These movements taught that the black man was God and that the Bible was a white man's book. They even taught that the white man ("the white devil," they called him) was created by a black rogue scientist named Yacob. Some of these teachings planted skepticism in my mind against the Bible, and I wasn't alone. Figures such as Malcolm X and Marcus Garvey, who became popular among black youth, also rejected the Bible because of such ideas. Young black teenagers began sporting African flattops along with beads and colors. The history and teachings of the Zulu tribe became popular among us, and Christianity was derided as a hoax. This was the environment that surrounded and influenced me during my impressionable early childhood.

In 1988 my family moved from the suburbs of Long Island, New York, to Fredericksburg, Virginia. My father had the opportunity to start in the real estate business there, and since it was an area without a lot of population, it promised quick growth. Sean and I were the only black kids in our new school—and the only New Yorkers, a fact in which we took great pride. The other kids looked at us like we were celebrities!

Virginia was quiet compared to New York City. Sometimes I felt like the silence was going to kill me! My brother and I practiced Wing Chun and danced to pass the time. I was a mediocre student who hated to study but was smart enough to do what I needed to get by. I thought of becoming a psychologist because I liked dealing with other people's minds.

In reality, I really had no plans for my future—no real goals or vision of what I wanted to do. Later that year, Sean Pollard, Vex, as we called him, moved to our area. He was a native of Brooklyn, and the three of us had an instant connection. It wasn't long before we decided to form a rap group because Vex was a lyricist, and we were hip-hop dancers. We began to enter talent shows and won all of them! That meant everything to us because now we were treated as stars! We also ended up in our share of fights with the local teenagers who didn't like the fact that we were popular.

In 1990 I graduated from high school and decided to go to college at Virginia State University in Petersburg, Virginia. While there, I began going by the name Africa. I was on my own for the first time in my life, and together with my roommate and his friends, I began experimenting with alcohol. College girls were also no longer living under parental watch, and they were everywhere. Classes didn't hold importance for me—besides, many of my classes required public presentations, and my fear of public speaking often kept me from attending.

I was also learning evil principles and becoming an astute student of the dark side, although I was largely ignorant of this fact. As a warrior of the dark side, I helped recruit others for acts of wickedness, drunkenness, violence, and rebellion. However, I was always careful to conceal these activities from my family. I was continually involved in gang fights in which I could have been killed or seriously maimed for life. Yet, somehow I was protected.

One night my brother Sean called me from Fredericks-burg. My parents were gone for the weekend, and he was home alone. He said that earlier that evening some kids that we didn't get along with had come to the house threatening him and daring him to come outside and fight. Five car-loads of my friends from Petersburg and Richmond drove up with me to Fredericksburg. My father had a collection of guns and rifles in his closet; we grabbed every one of them and went to the house of one of their crew. My friends sur-rounded the house, hiding behind bushes with guns cocked, while two of us went to the door. To this day, I thank God no one was home to answer the door!

In college, after long nights of partying, womanizing, fighting, and drinking, I would lie on my bed at night, won-dering, *What would happen if I died tonight? What would happen if I died without any knowledge of who God is or what He wants of me?* By day I was cool. But by night, when no one was looking or listening, these thoughts haunted me. In the stillness, when every other voice was silenced, a whisper from some unseen kingdom would call my name and speak to my soul. This Voice brought thoughts of eternity into my mind, calling me to consider my eternal destiny. But at the time I thought I merely was communicating with myself.

One evening I was at a friend's house, listening to music. Suddenly he exclaimed, "Man, you've gotta hear this song!"

As the music began to play, my interest was aroused. It was a melodic, repetitious sound. Then a voice began speak-ing; it sounded like the voice of the devil. It was quoting a verse from the Bible: "And I beheld when he had opened the sixth seal, and, lo, there was a great earthquake; and the sun became black as sackcloth of hair, and the moon became as blood; and the stars of heaven fell unto the earth, even as a fig tree casteth her untimely figs, when she is shaken of a mighty wind. And the heaven departed as a scroll when it is rolled together; and every mountain and island were moved out of their places" (Revelation 6:12–14).

As I listened to the voice of the devil reading what I thought might be Scripture, I had a sudden interest to read it for myself. Shortly after this, our whole crew, high on marijuana, gathered one night at a friend's house to read the entire book of Revelation!

Sean and Vex graduated from high school in 1991. Vex joined me at Virginia State, while my brother attended Virginia Union, only half an hour away. During that year, Mondo McCann, a native of the Bronx, New York, and also a student at Virginia State, joined us to form a four-member group that began performing at talent shows at different colleges. We almost always won first prize, and we were beginning to achieve stardom on campus.

Ivor and Sean Brooklyn, New York. 1979.

Ivor (Yoda), Mark (a cousin), and Sean (Jedi), Queens, New York. 1994.

3
PUPILS OF THE DARK SIDE

In the spring of 1992 I was attacked in the college cafeteria by the entire Virginia State University football team. Of course, the problem was over a girl—the girlfriend of one of the football players. She had broken up with him, and I had become briefly involved with her. Nothing physical had taken place between us, but the athlete was convinced that something had occurred.

He approached me as I was getting my food. "I heard you were trying to talk to my girl."

"What?" I replied. "You're not even together. Don't come at me with that!"

I was at least four inches taller than he was, but he outweighed me by at least eighty pounds. He was a senior, and I was only a freshman. But I had no fear. I had studied martial arts for years, and I also had watched Bruce Lee take out whole gangs on television!

"If I see you around my girl again, we're gonna fight," his eyes flashed fire.

Unmoved, I responded, "Whatever!"

As our voices began to get louder, a few of his friends

separated us, and I turned my back on him and walked away.

"What was that about?" a friend asked as I sat down at the table.

"Nothing," I responded nonchalantly. Just then I heard a noise behind me. I turned to see him coming up behind me, reaching for my neck! Jumping quickly to my feet, I assumed my Bruce Lee stance when all at once I realized that at least twenty members of the football team were with him!

That day I learned that life is not always what Hollywood makes it out to be. Immediately I found myself in the middle of a pile of football players throwing fists of fury. There really wasn't much I could do. I resigned myself for the demolition job to begin. However, more than human warriors were at battle that day. While evil angels were goading all of us on, the God of heaven, with whom I was not even acquainted, mercifully dispatched angels from the throne of light to engage in the conflict. Strangely enough, I didn't suffer even one blow. Within minutes of the attack, I found myself outside the cafeteria unscathed! But instead of being thankful for still being in one piece, I was seething with anger. It was time to make some phone calls. It was time for revenge!

The first phone call went to T—my best friend since the second grade. He was a student at neighboring Virginia Union College, the same school my younger brother Sean was attending.

"T!"

"What's up, Africa," he replied.

"We've got beef. Round up the 'crew.' Call Sean, and I'll meet you in an hour."

The next call I made was to my older brother Rhoan, all six feet eight inches, two hundred sixty pounds of him! He immediately started on the hour-long drive to the campus. And last, I called my own "crew" at Virginia State University. Later that night, about eighty or more of us stormed the college grounds searching for the football team. We were ready to do serious damage!

When we tried to get into the football team's dorm, a riot ensued, and the police were called out. Even after being chased by the police, about twenty of us made it into the dorm. We knew we were outnumbered, but we decided we would at least try to get into one dorm room. We found a room with an open door; the lights were off. All twenty of us barged into the room and slammed the door. Rhoan flicked on the lights. Two big burly roommates lay in their beds, surprised and perhaps wondering if this was a bad dream. We had pipes and other weapons in our hands. My brother towered over the two men in bed and told them to take a good look at me.

"The next time you think about touching him," Rhoan said, "you're going to be as good as gone."

Then we quietly slipped out of the room before the rest of the sleeping dorm realized what had happened. A day later, I was arrested by campus security and charged with trespassing, but because I was a college student, I was given a light sentence of community service.

This was normal life for me. In fact, it was part of the hip-hop package. The culture was having its effect on me. In baggy pants and hooded shirts, with red dreadlocks, I looked as rugged as possible. My friends and I often ended up in gang fights, bragging and boasting afterward about the thrill of the event.

The last thing occupying my mind was school. Music, women, and fame were the all-consuming passions. Every Friday night our "crew" would spend about an hour and a half preparing for the weekend festivities by steady drinking, while the rhythmic drums of the kings of hip-hop pulsated from car and house stereos.

A Virginia State University rap group, Das Effects, had just signed a record deal, and the whole campus was astir waiting for the group to release an album with hip-hop legends EPMD. Meantime, there was no doubt in my mind or in the minds of my friends that our turn at stardom would soon arrive.

The four of us—Mondo, Vex, Sean, and I—collectively known as The Boogie Monsters, were already making "noise" on the campuses around Richmond and Petersburg. Mondo and Vex took the microphone, while Sean and I performed a combination of martial arts and hip-hop dancing. After beating all the competition in our area, we turned our eyes to Washington, D.C., to enter the Howard University talent show that winter. This would be our biggest challenge. From our high-schools days we had snatched first place in almost every event, and now we would be going up against a wide range of contestants.

I fit the role of my assumed persona, Yoda, well. I was the one in search of hidden wisdom. Malcolm X had been one of my heroes from my youth, and I had always wanted to copy him—if not in doctrine, then at least in spirit. People even said that I looked like him! I fed my mental and spiritual energies on whatever I could glean from Islam, New Age, ancient Egyptology, or even *Star Wars*. After all, the hip-hop culture is not without its "spiritual" dimension.

When the time came for the Howard University talent show, we made the two-hour trip in an unheated Volkswagen Fox in the middle of winter. To make matters worse, we had no place to spend the night, so we slept (dozed is more like it) in the car in the freezing Washington, D.C., weather. The next day, with barely any sleep, we prepared for the contest. To our surprise, out of thirty contestants, we were scheduled to be the first act! This put us at a great disadvantage, because earlier acts were more likely to be forgotten by the end of the show.

After our performance we sat in the audience, watching every act to see if anyone had done better than we did. The competition was close. The winners were announced beginning with the third runner-up. We dreaded, and at the same time hoped, that our group would be called. If we couldn't win the contest, third place would be better than nothing. We were not the third runner-up. Relief or anguish? We were uncertain. The second runner-up was announced. Still not us! Then the announcer named the first-place winner. When he called out our name—The Boogie Monsters—we were relieved, but we kept our cool. We accepted the honor with a show of confidence as though we had known all along that we would win, that we were better than anyone else there!

That night, celebrity status became a sweet reality. We were interviewed, cheered, and applauded. It was this talent show that eventually led to our major record deal with EMI Records. Years of training under Satan, the prince of this world, the emperor of the dark side, had honed our desire for fame, worship, money, and the pleasures of this world. We were well on our way to the heart of the dark empire.

Ivor, Mom, and Sean. Virginia, 1989.

Sean Pollard (Vex) and Sean Myers (Jedi), pose with Ivor (Yoda) in 1990. Vex and Jedi have just graduated from high school.

4
STAR WAR ON I-95 NORTH

I woke up. How long had I been sleeping? I didn't know. This becomes even more significant to me today as I look back at that whole night. About 9:00 A.M. I had received a call from my cousin Susan, a native of England whom I had not seen in some time.

"Susan?"

"Yes, it's me," she replied, excited to hear my voice, as well. "I'm in New York for a few days on some business, but I need to speak to you and Sean tonight."

I sensed it was something important. "Do you want me to get in touch with Sean and call you back?"

"No, I need to speak to you both in person," she answered.

"OK, Susan; we'll be there!" It is roughly a six-hour drive from Virginia to New York, but sensing the urgency in her voice, I asked no questions. Leaving the campus, I picked up my brother at Virginia Union and off we went up Interstate 95.

That's when it happened! The bumps had brought me out of a mysterious sleep. I woke up and realized I was still in the car. I noticed that my hand was still on the steering wheel. I thought to myself, *This is strange!* I looked to my right, trying to get a sense of where I was, only to find that Sean was sleeping, as well. I looked down at the speedometer. It read seventy miles per hour. Then I looked at the road. There was no road. Still trying to get my bearings, I noticed branches hitting the windshield. Bewildered, I finally looked to my left and saw the highway that I *should* have been on!

How long I had been driving on the shoulder of the highway, I don't know. A few feet closer to those trees and a sure death would have been the result. Without panicking, I simply steered the car back onto the highway.

It wasn't until I got to New York early the next morning that I realized the full significance of what had happened. After greeting my cousin and spending a few minutes in conversation, I saw her face turn serious. I knew she had something important to say. In a sincere, urgent tone, she said, "The Lord wants both of you to give your lives to Him and be baptized!"

I was taken aback. Susan had always talked to us about the Bible, and we respected her very much. But she was never pushy, so this announcement came as a surprise. But instead of feeling offended, a sense of urgency swept over my brother and me.

"If you guys were to die tonight, where would your souls go?" Susan asked.

I realized my soul surely would not be with God! Her question was that strange one that had haunted me from childhood: *What happens to people when they die?* And other questions followed: *Where do people go when they die? Why do the wicked have to burn in hell forever, and how is that fair? How can I even be sure there is a heaven or a hell?*

With loving urgency, Susan continued, "Please, would you both consider giving your lives to Christ and getting baptized?" I felt as though God was speaking directly to me. I didn't know how to react. *Give my life to the Lord?* I had too many things to do with my life—like becoming famous. As we talked, it suddenly hit me: *What about the mysterious sleep that came over us the night before? Why didn't we crash?* Something inside me began to see that our mysterious sleep was no coincidence. If Satan and evil spirits existed, this must have been an encounter with them! If my cousin was a God-sent invitation, then what had happened had to have been the devil trying to take our lives before we arrived.

Bone chilling questions started to flood my mind. *Could it have been the devil that tried to kill us so we would not receive this invitation?* I knew that I couldn't have defended myself from evil angels bent on my destruction, even if I *were* awake! *Were these demonic star warriors trying to snuff out our lives knowing that this visit would be a major turning point for us? Could it have been God's holy warriors who had intervened, taking that steering wheel and keeping us from harm as we slept? Could this have been our own star war going on while we slept?* At that moment I heard the faint but powerful voice of the Holy Spirit, as though He was calling me by name.

I had heard about angels and how they sometimes intervened in the affairs of human beings. There was the time as a toddler that I was almost kidnapped from the beach. Being a fair-skinned baby on the beaches of Jamaica, I was an irresistible sight for a white couple who had scooped me up from my carriage while my mother was in the water. "Something" told her to turn around, and she did so in time to see the tip of my blanket disappearing in the distance. She began to scream, and my uncle took off after the couple and caught them. Perhaps it was an angel that told her to turn around and where to look.

When I was about four, I was traveling with my mother and younger brother on a train where the last car was not enclosed. We were on that last car, and I was at the edge while my mother and Sean were walking down the aisle to be seated. Suddenly, without warning, the train began to move. It lurched forward, causing me to lose my balance and fall off the back of the car. Almost immediately, the train began to back up! My mother had turned just in time to see me fighting in vain to keep my balance. Then out of nowhere a man appeared and caught me before I hit the ground, moving me out of harm's way! To this day my mother cannot recall who the man was or what happened to him afterward. It very well could have been an angel.

And then there was the gun incident. My cousin and I were twenty and eighteen years old at the time. We were sitting no more than six feet apart as he played with a pellet gun he thought was unloaded. As we talked in the living room, he aimed the gun at my head twice and playfully pulled the trigger. It was the ricochet of a piece of the wall the second time he pulled the trigger that made me turn around. That's when we saw the pellet holes in the wall on either side of my head. *Did an angel guide those bullets to safety?* I knew that I could have been seriously injured or killed, but I never thought to assign this work to angels.

Now, for the first time in my life, I wondered if God cared so much about me that He had intervened by taking the steering wheel while I slept. Had He spared my life for a purpose? The next day, Sean and I drove back to Virginia in awe. *Could it be true? Did we have a meeting with angels?*

As a result, I began to look for a way to calm my fears, leading to my first "born-again" experience, if one could call it that. There was a young man on campus whom everyone had made fun of continually. He was a Christian, and he was always wearing a Walkman, listening to the Bible and religious songs. He didn't have "in" clothing like everyone else, and most people thought He was weird for being into Jesus.

All of us poked fun at him, but my cousin's urgent plea to give my life to Jesus and be baptized had changed me. One night I paid this Christian a visit, making sure no one saw me. I had one question on my mind: "What do I have to do to be saved?" He led me through a series of Bible texts and then asked me if I wanted to let Jesus into my heart. I timidly replied that I did, and he asked me to repeat a prayer after him. I did, and I felt like a load of guilt was taken off my shoulders. Now I could party! And if I happened to die, I'd be saved! That's what I thought then.

Shortly after this, I saw the dead body of a woman who had been the victim of a drug-related stabbing. I was one of the first on the scene, and I thought, *This lady was unprepared to die.* I still didn't understand what happened to a person when he or she died. I wondered if this woman was looking down or *up* at her own body. This was troubling. *I must get baptized,* I thought. *I must not die unprepared!* Again, at that moment, I heard the whisper of the Spirit of God call my name.

The next day I went all around Petersburg, looking for a church that would baptize me. I didn't bother to check the denomination of the church. All that mattered was that I be baptized. Any church that offered to study with me, I refused. I had to be baptized immediately! I finally found a Baptist church that would baptize me without study. That Sunday, my brother and I were buried together in the watery grave—alive. Our lives hadn't changed in the least; all that this church asked of us was a profession of faith.

Now I really felt that if I died amid a fight or at a party, everything would be all right. Sean and I came up out of the water as wet sinners, ready to continue life on the dark side. Little did we realize that these events were only small battles in a larger war that was being fought over our souls—and over the souls of every other living person on planet Earth. We didn't see this as a battle to save us from the black hole, the powerful capital of the dark empire. After all, we had spent most of our lives there and were preparing at that very moment to go even deeper into a black hole that had claimed millions of captives—a black hole from which none ever return apart from the power of Christ.

Cousin Susan. Fredericksburg, Virginia, 1990.

5
ENTER THE
BLACK
HOLE

The Boogie Monsters were determined to get a record deal, and all the work we had put into our music, all the missed classes, and all the talent shows looked as though they were finally paying off. We were truly determined to do whatever it took to make this happen.

Once we were on Interstate 95 headed to Hampton, Virginia, to record our demo tape. On the way, we got lost and found ourselves on a one-way road that ended at a ferry. The traffic behind us forced us to drive onto the ferry, and when we got off on the other side, we were irritated and ended up in an argument. But we pressed on determinedly. After reaching the other side, the rest of the trip was made in silence. Then, without warning, the left rear tire of my Volkswagen Fox blew out. Silently, I pulled over. No one said a word. We had no spare. *Things can't get much worse*, I thought.

Then, from what seemed like a clear blue sky, a torrent of rain began to fall! Seconds later, a large truck drove past, and the force of the wind it created removed my back passenger window, which was a light plastic replacement. We

all sat there, expressionless, water beating down on the oc-
cupants of the backseat.

Determined, we decided to hitchhike the rest of the way.
The man who picked us up was in the military and harassed
us, boot camp style, the whole time about not having a
spare, traveling so late, and being lost. He even seemed irritated that he had picked us up!

Despite all this and many other trying circumstances, we
pressed on and were able at last to record the tape. No obstacle could keep us from doing whatever it took to become
famous. Every day a record deal seemed a little closer. And
then it happened. The night we won the major talent show
at Howard University, someone approached us and offered
to help us fund a new four-song demo that would be shopped
around the major recording labels in New York!

We went to work immediately. The sooner we could get
out of school the better! We had no other plans than being
famous. Our classes just didn't matter. The Boogie Monsters wanted to make an impact in the world. At the time,
"gangsta rap" was at its height. But we wanted to do something "positive" with our music. For Sean and me, our recent baptism also gave our music a *slightly* spiritual tone. In
a short time we laid the tracks and lyrics for four songs, and
soon we were ready to take the tape to New York.

This was 1994. At college, the summer break was arriving, and the campus was sensing that something big was on
the horizon for our group. There was a buzz on campus just
as there had been a year before with the group Das Effects.

After we finished our demo tape, we received an invitation to meet with a possible production and management
team who would professionally shop our music. The four of
us eagerly made the trip to New York City. The sound of

honking horns and the smell of Italian pizza was a welcome-home salutation for us. We were ready to replant our roots in the big city.

What an experience it was to walk into the famed Rush studio out of which Fran and her partner D worked. It was here that so many hip-hop legends had been introduced to the world—Run-D.M.C., LL Cool J, and many others. We were walking into the fantasy world we had dreamed of since childhood.

After producing the tape, we sat and watched intently as the management team listened. We knew from their faces that they were impressed. After listening, they told us they felt confident that they could get us a deal. Before we left the studio, we signed a contract with them to promote our demo, and within six days we received a phone call to meet at Pendulum/EMI Records for an interview with the president of the label.

The record company's offices were in a high-rise building on Sixth Avenue, where we met, talked, and even performed for the president of the company. The outcome? An eight-album, $800,000, record deal, with money rising in increments for each album! When we were left alone for a moment, the four of us began jumping up and down on the tables screaming in silence. *No more school,* I kept thinking. We were going to be label mates with rising stars like Lords of the Underground and Digable Planets. We were going to be stars alongside our own heroes of the hip-hop culture.

But there was one last obstacle that Sean and I had to face—our parents! Strict believers in education, Mom and Dad protested when we asked to drop out of school to follow a career in the entertainment industry. We argued our case but to no avail. It was not until our managers produced the evidence of a record deal and the fame that was sure to come that Mom and Dad decided to allow us to take a semester off as a trial run. If things didn't work out, we would go back to school.

We agreed, knowing in the back of our minds that we would *never* have to return to school. The Boogie Monsters were well on their way to the center of a black hole.

The Boogie Monsters' album Riders of the Storm: The Underwater Album *was released in 1994. Pictured on the back cover are Mondo, Jedi, Yoda, and Vex.*

At the album release party (left to right): Shadow, Yoda, Lee, Vex, Mondo, T, and Jedi.

6
LIGHT ENTERS THE DARK EMPIRE

Stepping into the unknown was an exhilarating feeling. My peers would finish their education, perhaps get a nine-to-five job, and live the life of an average person, having only a small circle of influence—friends, family, and co-workers. For the four of us, however, the future was now brilliant with adventure, excitement, stardom, and the exciting possibilities of the unknown.

It was risky business to drop out of school and give up the promised security of a college education. But we were about to leave it all behind. It was a step of faith. Our future was like the thrilling unpredictability of a storm, and we were ready for the adventure. Who knew where success was about to take us?

So, that summer of 1994 we said our Goodbyes to college classmates and were off for New York City. We didn't go alone. Many of our friends came with us. We were hoping to get a record deal for them also. Within our circle were three singing groups. We were collectively known as the Riders of the Storm, or X-men, and our pact had been that whoever was the first to secure a record deal would in turn help the others.

We soon secured a large four-bedroom house in Queens. From there we traveled by train to Manhattan to begin recording our first album, *Riders of the Storm*, so called from the famous song by the rock group The Doors, "Riders on the Storm." Their abstract style had made them an idol among us.

About twenty to thirty friends could be found in our house at any given time. We had no curfew and no worries; we were like a big family. Our whole "crew" sported dreadlocks and baggy clothing; we indeed looked like boogie monsters. We were all like brothers. One evening we made our unforgettable "Brotherhood Stew." Placing a big pot of soup on the stove, everyone (about thirty of us) brought different ingredients. It was a symbolic dinner representing our friendship. Though we were all different, we considered one another special friends, each bringing some different flavor to the crew. We wrote music together, smoked marijuana together, and partied together.

Marijuana and alcohol became a part of the routine. At times so much traffic went through our house that I would step over people I didn't know, sleeping on my floor. But it was all fun. Traveling back and forth to the studio on the subway, the smell of the city—all of it was novel. We were living the life we had always seen on TV.

We would often run into Busta Rhymes or A Tribe Called Quest or some of the other heavyweights of hip-hop. We were also to be fellow musicians with then rising stars such as The Fugees, The Roots, Souls of Mischief, The Pharcyde, and Da Bush Babees. Despite our record deal, we were still very much fans of the hip-hop greats. We were now at the heart of the black hole, a part of the mysterious force stars have over ordinary people. This force had drawn us to its core. Others were privileged to feel only the effects of the force; we would get to become a part of it. Through our music we could now influence the minds of young people, as our favorite stars had influenced us.

We began recording *Riders of the Storm*, and a buzz had already hit the streets about our four-member group. We worked meticulously on the album, spending many hours in the studio. We wanted a unique sound, a unique style. Our philosophy was that hip-hop was becoming watered down, generic, and without substance. Groups were either too abstract to understand or too simple to be of any depth. We wanted to bring a new breadth and depth to hip-hop. This led to songs like "Old Man Jacob's Well," a role-playing song about a child murderer who thinks he is helping children by taking them out of this evil world, and "Recognized Thresholds of Negative Stress" which portrays the danger of stress and the benefits of having a carefree spirit. Our ideas made the group outstanding from the beginning. And as word started to get out about our group, the interviews began to come in, as well. Magazines such as *Rolling Stone*, *VIBE*, and *The Source* wanted to tell the entertainment world about this new group. Photo shoots, free clothes, and limousines were now becoming a normal part of our lives. From coast to coast we were being touted as revolutionary in a hip-hop world that had lost its focus.

On October 2, 1994, *The New York Times* carried the following article, titled "Boogie Monsters: 'Riders of the Storm: The Underwater Album.' " "The Boogie Monsters were discovered last year at Howard University's annual rap competition. 'Riders of the Storm: The Underwater Album,' the groups debut album, has been winning fans because of the flippant attitude of the rhymes, the unpolished playfulness of the music and the oddball, but memorable choruses. The raps are abstract, stream-of-consciousness tone poems, far removed from the crime stories served up by gangster rappers."

The *San Francisco Bay View* (then called the *New Bayview*) on September 2, 1994, carried this article by David Alston: "Boogie Monster Debut Refreshing Mix of Cool." "I'm not surprised that the label that brought us *Arrested Development* and *Digable Planets* is releasing the debut by the *Boogie Monsters*. What does surprise me is why they waited so long . . . these four guys rap a message that lasts." Yes, we were destined for greatness. Life was what we thought it should be.

There was no shortage of new friends and acquaintances. One new acquaintance in particular stands out. I remember the first time I met D. He had grown up with one of my friends, Andrew, whom I had met at Virginia State University. Andrew had invited D over to our house one day, and we hit it off well. D was one of us. He had dreadlocks like us, and he smoked marijuana with us, but he would not drink alcohol. There was something different about him, but I couldn't tell what it was. He seemed to be wiser than his nineteen years.

At first I thought he might be a Rastafarian. Rastafarianism is a peculiar religion that teaches that former Emperor of Ethiopia Haile Selassie I was a twentieth-century manifestation of God. It arose as a rebel cry from the Jamaican slaves and grew to become one of the dominant religious forces of the hip-hop world. This religion uses marijuana as a key to meditation and more intense communication with God. Dreadlocks are a symbol of the religion. Its roots are in the teachings of Marcus Garvey, a black Jamaican nationalist who taught black power and initiated the Back-to-Africa movement in the early 1900s. Marcus Garvey taught that a black king would be crowned and become the deliverer of the black race. Many thought the prophecy was fulfilled when in 1930, Ras Tafari was crowned Emperor Haile Selassie I of Ethiopia and proclaimed "King of Kings," "Lord of Lords," and "Conquering Lion of Judah" as some of his titles. The Rastafari movement gets its name by combining the word *Ras,* which means "Head" or "Duke" or "Chief," and the name of Tafari Makonnen, which is the pre-coronation name of Haile Selassie I. Haile Selassie claimed to be a direct descendent of King David, the 225th ruler in an unbroken line of Ethiopian kings from the time of Solomon and Sheba. It was popular to be Rastafarian, especially in the hip hop culture and among the young men in New York City, and I thought this was perhaps the case with D. In fact, being from Jamaica, my brother and I had strong leadings toward Rastafarianism, which was also reflected in our music.

One night, we were all in the basement of our house smoking marijuana and just hanging out. The conversation began to move from light, trivial things to spiritual ideas. Back at Virginia State University we had all gone through something of a spiritual metamorphosis with our music. Influenced by rock artists such as Jim Morrison (The Doors), Pearl Jam, Nirvana; rap musicians such as De La Soul and A Tribe Called Quest; and reggae artists such as Yellowman, Bob Marley, and others, we too wanted to leave a dent in the music industry. We would combine abstract music and abstract spirituality and apply them to hip-hop. To do this we would use a combination of Christianity, Rastafarianism,

Eastern mysticism, African-based religions, and whatever else we could get our hands on. We represented a melting pot of religious ideas.

In a sense, hip-hop had already begun to combine the teachings of Christianity with Rastafarianism and a host of other African and Egyptian religions to come out with its own hybrid form of spirituality. Because of this, I studied these religions and steeped myself in black-power teachings.

Tonight, among the din of music, smoke, and invisible demonic forces, our conversation centered upon the Bible. Just as a conflict between angelic hosts had taken place earlier in our lives over Sean and me on I-95, this night I would again feel the presence of a spiritual conflict in unseen realms. Once again, angels were taking their places on the battlefield of my heart. Looking back, I can now see that if the fallen star warriors could get us to take the words of the Bible lightly, they would at least have had more time to influence and train us to possibly reject the words of truth we were about to hear. If they could keep this young man, D, quiet or occupy his mind with other things, perhaps the words would not be spoken at all. On the other hand, if angels of light could encourage D to speak, and if we accepted the words that they knew were planted in D's mind, the hold of fallen angels over us would begin to be broken. A group of promising students of the dark side would rebel against the empire and join the ranks of Jesus Christ.

The war began as we found ourselves in a conversation about last-day events. This grabbed everyone's attention, especially in light of the fact that a few months earlier, over twenty of us (high on marijuana) had gathered to read through the book of Revelation in one night. To counter the influence of the conversation, demonic "stars" tried to encourage us to take more puffs of marijuana. Perhaps the weed could get to our minds before the words. Angels of light moved upon D to speak. "When do you guys think the Sabbath is?"

The question sideswiped us. *What does this have to do with last-day events?* I thought. It seemed such a stupid question and out of place. What did the Sabbath have to do with the book of Revelation?

"Sunday," we responded.

"Everyone knows that," I said, totally forgetting about my conversation with my uncle years earlier.

"Think again," D countered. "Which day is the first day of the week?" We thought for a moment. Some responded, "Sunday," others "Monday." Once we got that straightened out with the help of a calendar, D continued, "Now what does the Sabbath commandment say?" He then proceeded to quote Exodus 20:8–11:

> Remember the sabbath day, to keep it holy. Six days shalt thou labour, and do all thy work: But the seventh day is the sabbath of the LORD thy God: in it thou shalt not do any work, thou, nor thy son, nor thy daughter, thy manservant, nor thy maidservant, nor thy cattle, nor thy stranger that is within thy gates: For in six days the LORD made heaven and earth, the sea, and all that in them is, and rested the seventh day: wherefore the LORD blessed the sabbath day, and hallowed it.

How in the world did this nineteen-year-old just quote that text from memory, I thought.

D continued, "The Sabbath is the seventh day of the week. Sunday is the first day. Saturday is the seventh day of the week, not Sunday. So, Saturday is the Sabbath."

I was dumbfounded. There in the midst of enemy territory, a spark of light touched my mind. Right there, at that very moment, amid smoke and pollution, a burning desire ignited within me like a match. If this were true, why did so many people go to church on Sunday? It was like stumbling upon a profound, hidden mystery. Wasn't this commandment one of the ten, given by God to this world? If so, what were the ramifications of not keeping one of them? What other truths were there in the Bible that I was ignorant of? In vain, unseen wicked star warriors fought to end the conversation. In vain, they attempted to change the subject! Almost all night we were mysteriously locked into this discussion about the Bible. I kept thinking to myself, *How does D know so much about the Bible, and how does he make it all so clear?*

In the days and weeks that followed, this scene was repeated. Night after night, for hours on end, our whole crew pored over God's Word amid the smoke of marijuana. The star wars intensified. The struggle was between fame and success on the one hand versus time for Bible study on the other. Bible study was quickly becoming as important to me as the desire for fame. This mysterious Book of the kingdom of light was becoming a new force in my life.

On the streets of New York, it is not unusual to run into different religious groups pushing their ideas—sometimes on the same street corner! I usually stopped to listen when I encountered such a group and accepted its publications to learn more about its beliefs. On one occasion, I received a little book from someone at a street corner. It was simple, but attractive, and the person handing it to me said that it was about Bible prophecy. Immediately, I was interested in reading it. To my surprise, many of the same things D had been sharing with us were in this book. I had thought D had discovered these things all by himself. Now I was surprised to learn that at least one other person—the author of this book—seemed to be on the same page with D!

Before long I was trying to get my hands on every religious book I could so I could learn more. But my main interest was the Bible itself. Poring over God's Word began to do something inside me. The vivid imagination I had so often used to imagine a world of my own creation was suddenly redirected. Some unseen power seemed to be beckoning me and inviting, "Imagine this." My imagination slowly began to take in the biblical picture: Satan had once been an angel on the side of light, the highest in God's kingdom. He was loved and honored. Most important of all, he was the angel who was closest to Jesus. They were the best of friends. Originally named Lucifer, he was the light bearer. Using a wicked king of an ancient kingdom as a symbol of Lucifer, the Bible declares,

Son of man, take up a lamentation upon the king of Tyrus, and say unto him, Thus saith the Lord God; Thou sealest up the sum, full of wisdom, and perfect in beauty. Thou hast been in Eden the garden of God; every precious stone was thy covering, the sardius, topaz, and the diamond, the beryl, the onyx, and the jasper, the sapphire, the emerald, and the carbuncle, and gold: the workmanship of thy tabrets and of thy pipes was prepared in thee in the day that thou wast created. Thou art the anointed cherub that covereth; and I have set thee so: thou wast upon the holy mountain of God; thou hast walked up and down in the midst of the stones of fire. Thou wast perfect in thy ways from the day that thou wast created (Ezekiel 28:12–15).

It was Lucifer's desire to usurp the throne of God. He began to feel that he deserved the worship that belonged to God. My imagination soared as I read these words:

How art thou fallen from heaven, O Lucifer, son of the morning! how art thou cut down to the ground, which didst weaken the nations! For thou hast said in thine heart, I will ascend into heaven, I will exalt my throne above the stars of God: I will sit also upon the mount of the congregation, in the sides of the north: I will ascend above the heights of the clouds; I will be like the most High (Isaiah 14:12–14).

Thou wast perfect in thy ways from the day that thou wast created, till iniquity was found in thee. By the multitude of thy merchandise they have filled the midst of thee with violence, and thou hast sinned: therefore I will cast thee as profane out of the mountain of God: and I will destroy thee, O covering cherub, from the midst of the stones of fire. Thine heart was lifted up because of thy beauty, thou hast corrupted thy wisdom by reason of thy brightness: I will cast thee to the ground, I will lay thee before kings, that they may behold thee (Ezekiel 28:15, 16).

My imagination took me back to that place and time described by the prophet. Like vivid colors on an artist's canvas, the scripture painted a baffling scenario. It was the ambitious wish of this brilliant angel to overthrow God's government. He clamored for a change in the laws of the kingdom of light. Believing in his own supremacy, believing that he was "like God," holy in himself, apart from God's power, Lucifer felt he no longer needed to submit to the laws of the city of light. In particular, his hatred and jealousy was aimed at the mighty Son of God. He began a deceptive campaign, pretending that he wanted to improve God's government. Through this act, Lucifer unleashed a mysterious force called sin, a force he did not fully understand. This force had subtly altered his mind, turning him into a master of deception. So insidious was his work that he deceived and recruited one-third of the angels in an attempt to take the throne and overthrow God as the Sovereign Ruler. "And there was war in heaven," the Bible says (Revelation 12:7). The dark side failed in its coup. The Son of God "beheld Satan as lightning fall from heaven" (Luke 10:18).

Lucifer and his warriors were cast out of heaven. After deceiving the first rulers of this world (see Genesis 3:1–7), Lucifer became the prince of this world. Here, he and his angels set up their new headquarters and their own laws. Here, they would continue to wage war against God, the Son of God, and the laws of the eternal city. They were a force causing pandemonium among humanity. And humanity needed a Hero! The thought carried my imagination into high gear. I wanted to learn more!

I learned that this entire biblical "star war" centered on God's law. Satan and his angels deceived human beings into disobeying God's government and His laws of light. Then Satan turned around and accused God of requiring an impossibility of His people, thus proving that He was an unjust ruler. To meet this challenge, the Son of God—the true "Sky Walker"—left the heavenly city of peace to take on human form, confronting Satan in his own dark empire. Here the Son of God proved that through Him, and only through Him, was righteousness and obedience to the law of glory possible. To thwart God's plan of salvation for humanity, Satan and his demonic warriors attempted to entice Jesus Christ, the Son of God, to choose the dark side and so bring Him under the mysterious force of sin.

This war against Jesus raged for thirty-three and a half years. Through seen and unseen warriors, the prince of darkness tried in vain to convert the Son of God to the force of darkness. In a climactic life-and-death battle, the two warriors met one last time in a place called Gethsemane. The entire forces of the dark empire converged on the Son of God in one final desperate effort. To no avail they press upon Him the cost of the sacrifice and the rejection He will face, even from His own Father. The conflict spilled over to a hill called Calvary. Here, through His heroic death and resurrection, the Son of God emerged as Conqueror over the forces of sin. Then He ascended to the city of glory. Honor, sacrifice, heroic death, a conflict of universal proportions! I wanted to yell for excitement as I had so many times before when creating my own heroic scenarios. This was the real thing, and no imagination!

I learned that Jesus' death and resurrection prepared the way for human beings to also enter through the gates of the city of glory. *Another world? An escape from this planet? Intergalactic travel?* I was beside myself in awe.

But there was more. The Bible pictured an innumerable company of people who would leave the dark side as a result of Jesus' victory and strike back against the evil empire. The death and victory of God's Son would give them "power to become the sons of God" (John 1:12). As warriors of light, their aim would be to prove that through Christ alone could one obey the law of God's kingdom and overpower the forces of darkness. They were to reveal what the grace of God could do in the life of a sinner. They were to prove that, contrary to Satan's theories, no one could be righteous on his own apart from God.

After his defeat at the Cross, Lucifer turned his wrath on Jesus' followers. "The dragon was wroth . . . and went to make war with the remnant . . . which keep the commandments of God, and have the testimony of Jesus Christ" (Revelation 12:17).

Satan knew that the Scriptures declare, "Blessed are they that do his commandments, that they may have right to the tree of life, and may enter in through the gates into the city" (Revelation 22:14). So, by attacking God's law, he hoped to deceive the world into disobedience. And he broadened his attack to question the very existence of God. Through his own list of formidable warriors, Charles Darwin, Hitler, and other renowned men of the world, Satan would try to reduce God's existence to a questionable theory.

As I became aware of these spiritual realities, I felt like Luke Skywalker, except that this was no movie! I began to wonder, *Is God calling me into this battle of universal proportions? Am I to be one of those innumerable star warriors, prophesied to help bring down the dark empire of Satan?* The thought was overwhelming and beyond anything I could have ever imagined for myself.

Yoda (center) discusses the mark of the beast and Adventism with a group of rappers on a video shoot. Atlanta, 1995.

Seated: Yoda and Vex on a video shoot. 1995.

7

A
DARK-SIDE
DECEPTION

In another prophecy, I learned that Satan would even use professed Christians to teach that the law of the eternal city, the Ten Commandments, has been done away with or altered in some way after the death of Christ. In the book of the ancient star warrior Daniel, a most amazing prophecy gripped my attention. The prophet describes the rise and fall of four ancient empires: Babylon, Media-Persia, Greece, and Rome (see Daniel 7). This description is followed by the breakdown of the Roman Empire into ten kingdoms represented by ten horns. The prophecy then speaks of a "little horn," a power that would think to change God's time and laws. "And he shall speak great words against the most High, and shall wear out the saints of the most High, and think to change times and laws" (Daniel 7:25).

This little horn symbolizes counterfeit Christianity, and how it would do the same work that Lucifer did in heaven. While professing to serve God and lead people to salvation, this power was actually attempting to "change" God's law. When I learned this, I was amazed. *If this is what the Bible is really saying, and if all this is really true, why haven't others seen this? If I can see it, why haven't others?* I almost felt as though I was in the twilight zone, or like Noah, living in a world full of people ignorant of truth. I would soon discover there were more people who understood these things than I could imagine!

As I talked further with D and learned Bible truth, it all made sense. God's law was never to be changed or altered, because it represented the unchanging nature of His character. In awe, I learned that God's Word even declared the reason the world was to be destroyed; namely, for changing and rebelling against the laws of the kingdom of light:

> Behold, the LORD maketh the earth empty, and maketh it waste, and turneth it upside down, and scattereth abroad the inhabitants thereof. . . . The land shall be utterly emptied, and utterly spoiled: for the LORD hath spoken this word. The earth mourneth and fadeth away, the world languisheth and fadeth away, the haughty people of the earth do languish. The earth also is defiled under the inhabitants thereof; *because they have transgressed the laws, changed the ordinance, broken the everlasting covenant. Therefore hath the curse devoured the earth*, and they that dwell therein are desolate: therefore the inhabitants of the earth are burned, and few men left (Isaiah 24:1, 3–6, emphasis supplied).

God wants us to be like Him in character. And this happens as we behold His perfect law that reveals our shortcomings and defects; then go to Jesus to be renewed, cleansed, and transformed into the likeness of God's character. I learned that human beings could be rescued, snatched from the dark side, and brought into fellowship with God.

I learned that one of God's laws that Satan has attempted to change is the Sabbath commandment. I was shocked to discover that only eight texts in the New Testament speak of the first day of the week and that not one of those eight state specifically that the Sabbath has been changed to Sunday.

As I learned more about God and the great battle going on between Jesus and Satan, I began to see my place in this "star war." The issue, as I saw it, was simple: Is it possible for a sinful human being to be so empowered by the grace of the King of the empire of light that he could be subject to the law of God even in a sinful world? *What a challenge*, I thought to myself.

After weeks of studying, we finally asked D what church he went to. "An Adventist church," he replied.

"A what?" I wanted to know.

"I am a Seventh-day Adventist," D replied.

"What is an Adventist?" I had never heard the name before. "What do they believe?" These questions filled my mind and the minds of everyone else in the crew. D told us that this was the church he attended and that he had been brought up in it. He was not fully following what the Adventists believed and taught, but I believe the holy angels were using him.

"We're going with you this Saturday to the Adventist church!" was the unanimous decision of the group. It was an amazing experience. That Sabbath, the first I had ever spent in an Adventist church, almost everyone in our crew entered the Laurelton Seventh-day Adventist Church—dreadlocks, gold jewelry, baggy pants, and all! If people looked at us strangely, we never noticed it. We were too busy trying to soak in everything the pastor was saying. Week after week, we attended the Laurelton church, even staying for the afternoon Bible studies.

I soon learned that there was a bookstore on Merrick Boulevard that sold Adventist books, and it became my second home. I read everything I could get my hands on. A series of little books by a ministry called Amazing Facts enriched my Bible study tremendously. I was blown away by what I was learning. I didn't own a Bible, so Mondo gave me one of his. It became my coloring book. As I read, I highlighted important passages using color codes.

Meanwhile, my brother was having his own personal encounter with Christ. Sean had been used to meditating through Rastafarianism. Now he was beginning to pray to God. After many secret prayer sessions, God was convicting him to follow what he had been learning from the Bible studies. Often, with tears in his eyes, Sean committed himself to God, to follow Him wherever He would lead.

I was impressed with D's ability to explain the Bible. It sparked a burning desire in me to be able to understand and share these truths myself. After going to church for a few weeks, we were introduced to something called "potlucks." After the service, the church would gather in the fellowship hall to enjoy a feast of various foods. It gave everyone time to fellowship together. I began to notice that there was never any meat on the table at these potlucks. As I continued to study, I soon understood why. I saw that God's original diet for Adam and Eve was fruits, nuts, and grains and that this diet was designed to keep us humans in optimal health. That's what I wanted for myself.

I don't believe it was a coincidence that the matter of diet came to my attention in November. Thanksgiving was coming up, and my family was a staunch consumer of all meat products. So, I knew that I was in for a challenge. But God's Word was clear, and I stopped eating unclean foods—on Thanksgiving Day!

I stuffed my stomach with rice and lettuce so I wouldn't feel that I had missed anything. I knew that if I could obey God on Thanksgiving Day, I would never turn back. And so it was. I also learned about some of the effects dairy products had on one's health. Ever since moving to Virginia as a teenager, I had suffered with asthma. But after a month or so of no dairy products, my asthma left. For months I ate like a bird; I knew nothing of such things as soymilk or other vegetarian products. I thought a vegetarian ate only vegetables, fruit, and nuts. And I was willing to make the sacrifice.

More convictions came as I continued to study and read. I began to discover things in my lifestyle that were not in harmony with the Word of God. Marijuana, for example. I slowly came to the conviction that smoking marijuana was a sin against God. I remember the day that some of us were in a heated conversation over the subject. "It's all right to smoke marijuana," someone argued, "because God blessed all herbs."

"But smoking is harmful; it destroys the temple of our bodies," Sean replied. "It can't be good."

"What about eating marijuana?" another interjected, "That way it doesn't harm the lungs."

For more than an hour we debated back and forth. Then some of us made up our minds: *No more marijuana!* Only

God's grace made it possible for us to conquer the habit. I knew the lack of control I had over my thoughts when under the influence of this drug. And since I knew that God wanted me to be clear minded at all times, I knew this drug couldn't be a blessing. Indeed, poisonous weeds and herbs came into the world as a result of sin, and marijuana is one of those.

Then one day Sean approached me and said, "You know, I've been convicted that as Christians, we shouldn't curse."

"What?" I exclaimed. "If I have to stop cursing, I'll never make it to heaven!" In our environment and culture, cursing was a part of our vocabulary, although we were careful of our language in the presence of our parents. It was an immense struggle to begin changing my language. But over time, and with God's grace working in my life, cursing left my vocabulary.

Meanwhile, my parents were becoming pleased with our success but they were unaware of our spiritual revolution. Money and fame were coming in. They saw that the record deal was a reality and decided we hadn't made such a bad decision after all. But at the very time that they were becoming reconciled to our hip-hop career, Sean and I began to approach them with what we were learning from the Bible. It was like hitting them with a sledgehammer. They thought we were losing our minds and becoming caught up in some weird movement. Our nonpraying parents actually began to pray for us! Yet, we pushed on, trying to convince them of what we were learning. We determined to follow Christ— with or without them.

Within a few short months, my friends and I were convinced that what we were learning from the Bible was truth, and we made a decision to submit ourselves to Jesus Christ.

The angel warriors of light had won a major conflict, and the angels of darkness had lost. We celebrated two mass baptisms. Half of our friends were baptized, and then a few weeks later, the other half went under the water. D was re-baptized, as he saw how God had worked through him in spite of his backsliding. Sean and I requested to be baptized together. It was the second time for us, but this time it was truly in spirit and in truth.

The name of our album was *The Underwater Album*. Satan was attempting to take us "underwater" and drown us in the sins of the black hole, but God had taken us underwater to experience the glories of the world to come, as John 3:5 affirms: "Verily, verily, I say unto thee, Except a man be born of water and of the Spirit, he cannot enter into the kingdom of God."

We were now star warriors of light. And the storm was about to become more intense than we had expected.

8

SHEEP
IN WOLVES'
CLOTHING

As we stood behind stage with microphones in our hands, we listened to the howling crowd. They were waiting for *us!* It was our opening-night album-release party. The legendary Red Alert was on stage introducing *us!* In the crowd were some famous rap groups who had been our idols. In the darkness, unseen angels of darkness mingled among the audience. Major changes had been happening in our lives. We had begun to follow Jesus, and we decided that we would let the world know about it. Make no mistake, the name of our group might seem to represent darkness, but The Boogie Monsters were going to let their new light shine!

Sean and I had been dancers up to this point, but we decided it would be irresponsible for us to have access to the world's ear and not speak about what we had learned. God had put a fire in our bones, and we could not keep silent. So, we exchanged our dancing for the microphone. *We would spread the three angels' messages through hip-hop.* Half our album was somewhat positive, but it was mingled with negative elements, as well. The second half had been recorded during our conversion experience and consisted of themes we had learned from the Bible. Ironically, we had named our album *The Underwater Album*, little realizing the significance of the name. Yes, The Boogie Monsters were on fire for God, and we had a message for the world.

As the lights went down, the auditorium went into total darkness. Dim red and blue lights now moved about as though in search for a stage presence, and an eerie Indian chant in the style of the '60s group The Doors echoed from the massive speakers. "Our Father which art in heaven . . ." The crowd went wild as it heard four voices repeating the Lord's Prayer over the speakers. It was time for us to experience a dream come true.

We had never planned to open our release party with the Lord's Prayer. But things had changed so rapidly for us. Now we saw ourselves as God's hip-hop group with a message for people as important as that which Moses delivered to Israel. We were like sheep, only in wolves' clothing. Our mission? To reach the world, mingle with the world, come in like wolves among wolves, and then reveal that we were actually sheep working for Christ.

"Hallowed be thy name. . . ." The crowded lifted their hands and made as if they were shooting guns in the air. "Thy kingdom come. Thy will be done in earth, as it is in heaven." The club was filled with alcohol and marijuana. We paid no attention to that. "Give us this day our daily bread. And forgive us our debts, as we forgive our debtors." Little did we realize the cosmic conflict going on over our souls that night. It was as though in this act we were ignorantly crying out to God to deliver us from an evil of which we were unaware. God heard those words: "And lead us not into temptation, but deliver us from evil." At that time we could scarcely imagine how that prayer would be answered. "For thine is the kingdom, and the power, and the glory, for ever. Amen."

That night, we were on top of the world. Our first song had hit the airwaves, and we were rubbing shoulders with those we had once reverenced on TV and radio. We felt God's presence with us. We felt we were prophets to a hip-hop generation that was alienated from God. We were on a mission.

The people who surrounded us didn't seem to mind our spirituality. Among our managers and representatives were atheists, a pagan, a witch, and homosexuals. They were all nice to us. None of them seemed to mind our Christian lyrics. We worked together, it seemed, in perfect harmony.

On one trip we flew out to California to perform on *Soul Train*. After the appearance, an interviewer asked us about our motivation for what we were doing. Unashamedly, we confessed Christ. I often thought about the shock people received when they saw how we looked—and then heard us confess that we were Christians. The two seemed like night and day. Sheep in wolves' clothing! But the public liked it. It was unique and daring, and they did not feel threatened by it at all. We were proud of our persona. We liked the shock effect. When we appeared on *Teen Summit*, we had Bibles in our hands while we performed. Our videos began airing on BET, MTV, and a host of other programs.

Before one live performance, I had been reading a book, *America in Prophecy* (also known as *The Great Controversy*). It outlined the prophecies of Daniel and Revelation. I came up with a plan. I made copies of certain pages and carried them onstage in my army-green backpack. During the performance, we asked, "Who wants to know about the prophecies of the last days?" Hands went up everywhere in the packed crowd. We started tossing these photocopied pages into the audience, and the people went after them wildly.

In our shows, we often spoke openly about God. In fact, we sometimes warned the audience that a time of destruction was coming for which they needed to prepare by putting away all their bad habits. *We considered ourselves shining lights in a dark empire; sheep in wolves' clothing.* We were on a mission to convert hip-hop. Our lyrics had gone from abstract to spiritual. Songs like "Mark of the Beast" now appeared on our album. We had a message for the people. My lyrics to "Red Dawn," an unpublished song, probed what would happen if Christ returned on the Sabbath, a Friday night, and how many people would be caught off guard in clubs and movie houses. The lyrics went like this

Red dawn. Look up in the sky.
Babylon is fallen; it's time for earth to die.
I stood upon the sand of the sea,
Seven thunders of the Almighty spoke a mystery,
Commanded me to look into the east and into the west,
And said, "Babylon must die, yes, in peace Babylon must rest.
Now lest you and your people be partakers of her sin,
Let the exodus from Babylonia begin."
And then, behold, the sixth seal was opened, and lo
The hand of the Almighty shook the foundations to and fro.
I counted seven plagues dissolving men everywhere,
and the hardest of the hard had their hearts stopped fear.
"Oh, My Lord," I cried. I cried, "When shall these things be?"
Then He led my mind to 2 Peter chapter 3.
So I read it, fell to the sand confused; I could not get it.
Then He said, "Let it not be said, that I would leave you dead."

Isaiah 58 verse 12 to 14 hit my head,
Knocked me down unconscious. . . . All I saw was Red . . .
Red dawn. Look up in the sky.
Babylon is fallen; it's time for earth to die.
I remembered Revelation chapter 7,
The angel said we needed the seal of God to enter heaven.
But what did this mean?
Wait! Isaiah 8:16 coincides with Exodus 31:17. Oh, my God!
"The day of the Lord will come like a thief in the night,"
If you knew, you just might keep His Sabbath.
Then I heard the voice of Job 34:20
telling me the omega would come at midnight upon many.
I trembled as I thought of how many would be discovered
out on Friday night, caught off guard, their sins uncovered!
Any who has wisdom, let him understand what's going on
"And pray that flight be not on . . . "
Red dawn. Look upon the sky.
Babylon is fallen; it's time for the earth to die!

When magazines like *VIBE* and *Rolling Stone* asked to
interview us, we would pack our interviews with Bible verses,
our philosophy of equality, and our desire to see a change in
hip-hop.

Once we were invited to participate in a panel discussion
at a Rainbow Coalition meeting with Jesse Jackson Jr. When
the microphones were turned over to us, we lifted up Christ
as the only solution to humanity's problems. We said that if
people were not willing to turn to Christ, the real issues of
racism would never end.

In my private time, I began a Bible study on the campus
of New York University. Strangely enough, my fear of talking in front of people subsided when I talked about the Bi-

ble. About thirty students who had never heard the truths of Scripture before were attending the study. Each week we went through the Bible, discovering the amazing truths of God's Word. Many of the Bible study students started attending church. I began to meet other young people from different denominations who would invite me to their churches. I gladly attended, wanting to talk to other Christians about the truths I was learning.

On one occasion, I attended a Church of Christ retreat in New Jersey where about a thousand people were present. A baptism was scheduled for that Sunday. A friend was to be one of those baptized. On a Friday afternoon, about an hour after I arrived at the retreat, I found myself surrounded by half a dozen people, including my friend who was to be baptized, while I talked to them about the Sabbath. At the end of that short Bible study on the Sabbath, my friend had decided he no longer wanted to be baptized. This aroused the anger of the retreat leaders.

The next day I found myself in the center of a hotel room surrounded by the church leaders and other spectators. It was like a scene out of a movie. They sat me down in a chair right in the center of the room. "Why are you insisting that we keep the old Jewish Sabbath? We're not under the law."

"Show me from the Bible where Sunday is the new day of worship, and I'll believe," I replied.

Immediately, one of the leaders jumped out and started abusing me verbally. "Look at you!" he shouted. "Nobody wants to be like you." I wondered what my appearance (dreadlocks and all) had to do with my theology. He continued for some time in a vain attempt to put me down in front of everyone. I made sure to keep calm so those in the room could see the difference of spirits! I was being interrogated for the Lord. I was being trashed—put down. In fact, I was surprised to find the church leaders speaking in the tones they did. *What a privilege,* I mused silently! *I am being persecuted for truth! Yes!!!!* So ruthless were my opponents that my friend, who was also present in the room, became firmly convinced that he would *not* be baptized there. He and I were thrown out of the retreat and had to hike back home. We rejoiced all the way.

One day while I was relaxing in our Brooklyn apartment, the phone rang. The voice on the other end of the line introduced himself and said he was in New York and wanted to meet with The Boogie Monsters. I didn't get his name and asked him to repeat it. He said, "My name is David Faustino."

"David who?" I replied.

"Bud Bundy," he finally said. "I'm Bud Bundy from the TV sitcom *Married With Children.*"

I couldn't believe it! "Bud!" I exclaimed, as though he were a long-lost friend.

"Yeah, you guys are my favorite hip-hop group, and I just wanted to meet you."

So, we arranged to meet at a restaurant in the Village. We talked for a long time. After a few hours, David began to share with me the emptiness he experienced in the entertainment industry. *We were two stars in the black hole of stardom.*

I began to share with him the truths I had been learning from God's Word. He began to share with me some things from his past and how he was searching for something deeper. That Sabbath David and I walked into the Kingsboro Seventh-day Adventist Church in Brooklyn, New York, where I had been baptized. Afterward, David told me how moved he was at the presence of God there. I have since lost contact with him, but I pray that God will lead him into the truth as He led me.

I was happy in my newfound ministry as "hip-hop prophet." After listening to some lyrics I had recently written about the second coming of Christ, a friend said to me, "Have you ever thought about becoming a preacher?"

"Nope," I said. "Besides, I'm already a preacher."

David Faustino, who played Bud Bundy on the TV sitcom Married With Children, *holds Ivor's daughter, Jaden. 1995.*

9

WAKING UP
IN THE
BLACK HOLE

The spiritual awakening in my life had brought me out of the darkness of ignorance concerning God's Word. I now had a clearer picture of the truths of Scripture and shared them readily and excitedly. The Boogie Monsters had converted from being a secular hip-hop group to a spiritual one. The December 1, 1995, issue of *Essence* magazine carried the following article: "Souls of Young Black Folks: Spirituality in the Nineties."

> *The Boogie Monsters* are hip hop messengers of Christ. While some groups rap about gold, girls, and guns, these newly converted Seventh-day Adventists urge listeners to "unite and do what's right" to avoid receiving the "Mark of the Beast," as a song on their 1994 CD *Riders of the Storm: The Underwater Album* is titled. "Entertainment is second," stresses one of the four rappers, (Ivor) "Yoda" Myers. "Our message comes first."

That was the truth. Our message had become our consuming theme. We wanted to make a change in the stream of hip-hop. And we were doing it. *VIBE* magazine, September 1994 wrote about what we were doing:

> With a sound falling somewhere between the Pharcyde and 3 Feet High and Rising-era De La Soul, Boogie Monsters—Mondo, Vex, Yoda, and Myntric—bypass blunts, beat downs and 9mm blasts. They rap about everything from women to the negative state of the world, and they have a delivery versatile enough to handle it all. The New York quartet's excellent debut maintains a near perfect balance of samples and live instruments. "Recognized Threshold of Negative Stress" is a clever freestyle flowing over a liquid baseline. "Mark of the Beast" checks on the devil while a loop of strings peaks and crashes. . . . Riders of the Storm brings 1989 to mind—back when Native Tongues, and Kwame made their way onto the scene, when hip hop wasn't about being hard, when it was about telling stories, getting deeper concepts across, and doing it in a way no one had done before. If The Boogie Monsters get the props they deserve on this effort, Riders might just be a turning point in hip hop.

The September 16 issue of the *Charlotte Observer* carried this piece: "You wonder, after listening to what could become a landmark disc, if this will send rappers on a new journey: one toward self discovery—and teaching—and away from praising gang war and dissing. Really this would be a journey back to the future. Rap really started out where the Boogie Monsters are headed."

Having entered this spiritual journey and being baptized, I had found a new significance in the latter half of our album title, *The Underwater Album.* We had gone underwater to experience newness of life, and our album reflected this conversion in a sense. But now I was to find significance also in the first part of our album title, *Riders of the Storm.* For the storm began in my own soul one weekday afternoon on a sunny day in the Pendulum office. We were reading letters sent to us by admirers and fans when we came across one that surprised us. I don't have this letter anymore, nor do I remember the writer's name. All I can say is that I pray I will meet this person at the gates of the Holy City someday.

Vex opened the letter and read it while the rest of us listened. The letter went something like this: "Dear Mondo, Vex, Yoda, and Myntric. I am a great fan of yours, and I appreciate your music. You are doing a great work for the hip-hop community. However, I have a question. You guys say that you are a rap group for God. The Bible says in Amos 3:3, 'Can two walk together except they be agreed?' And 2 Corinthians 6:14 says, 'For what fellowship hath righteousness with unrighteousness? and what communion hath light with darkness?' The Bible also points out that we should 'abstain from all appearance of evil' (1 Thessalonians 5:22). In light of these scriptural truths, how can you have a name like The Boogie Monsters and yet profess to serve God?"

We had never stopped to think about it. In fact, no one had ever questioned us in this way. We all dismissed the letter as just some crazy fan. But that night I couldn't sleep. A storm was brewing in my soul. The writer of that letter was right. How could we claim to represent God and keep a name that was obviously a name of darkness? But would our record label let us change the name of the group even if we tried? And if they didn't, what would we do then? How were we going to ride this storm?

The following day the four of us brought up the matter. After discussing it for some time, we decided that we would ask to change our name to Riders of the Storm. We would call a meeting with our managers and the label company and make the request. *After all, they are all really nice people,* we thought. When we met, however, they flatly denied our request. We were told that the name The Boogie Monsters was unique, and it stuck. It was too late to change it. We explained our reasons and convictions, but we didn't make even a dent in their decision. We decided that we would make the best of it and turn the name into a spiritual meaning. From now on The Boogie Monsters would come to represent being afraid of something or someone that a person doesn't understand. After all, we reasoned, "normal" people were afraid of us or judged us because of our appearance, but little did they know that we were Christians! Serious Christians. This is the angle we would use. Our managers bought it, our fans bought it, and my conscience quieted for a time. But the storm did not subside. I began to notice other dark forebodings regarding the direction we were headed. It wasn't long before the storm hit in all of its fury.

As performers we were often on the road, and the weekend was our biggest venue. At first, we didn't see a problem with Friday night performances—after all, we were performing for God. But as I went over in my mind the conflict over the name of the group that continued to brew in my soul, I began to notice other danger signs. We were touring in California. It was a Friday. Back and forth we went, studying the Bible and praying, "Lord, is it all right to perform for You on the Sabbath? We are doing Your work, and though the people are paying to come and see us, we are giving them the three angels' messages." We weren't able to come to a decision, so we decided we would ask God for a sign.

That night we had four scheduled appointments—three radio interviews and a live performance. We prayed in the presence of friends, road managers, and everybody, "Lord, if You don't want us to perform on Sabbaths anymore, please cancel all four of our appointments tonight. Amen."

In all our time of touring, it had been a rarity for us to have even one cancellation. Now we were asking God to do an incredible feat and cancel four appointments in one night—and a Friday night!

The time came for our first radio interview. When we got to the station, the radio manager told us that something had happened, and there wouldn't be an interview that night. All of us and our entourage looked at one another in bewilderment. All our faces carried the same expression: "No way!"

As we piled back into the limousine and headed to our next radio interview, we talked about the odds of that first interview being canceled. We were intensely anticipating arriving at our next destination. When we got there, we were told the interview was going to be canceled! By this time, we felt like we were in the twilight zone—no, we were in the black hole, and God was trying to pull us out!

We arrived at our third radio interview, and no one showed up! All that was left now was the live club performance. We had never had a show canceled before. This would be it. If the show was canceled, we would know for sure that God was calling us to stop performing on Sabbath. But then, I began to think, *What will happen when we approach the label company and request not to perform on Sabbath? What if they say No?* Suddenly, the storm in my soul picked up velocity and fury.

When we got to the club, we were told that the show had been canceled! God had done the impossible—the incredible! The God who opened the Red Sea for the children of Israel and who had made time stand still for Joshua had made a straight path for us. By shutting down all four of our performances that night in answer to our fervent prayer, He revealed His will to us. Again the ball was in our court. We must face the label company again. We must tell the executives, firmly this time, that we would not perform on Sabbaths. End of question.

We set up the meeting and presented our conviction and that we had decided not to perform on Sabbath. The record company executives thanked us for such a noble commitment, and the meeting adjourned with an unspoken warning: Perform or the deal ends! *What happened to the nice people I knew? Could this just be all about the money? Didn't they encourage our Christian hip-hop stance?* They backed away from the storm and postponed taking a definite stand. But in an effort to quiet our consciences, we decided we would not take any money from our Friday night shows. But now another storm began to brew in my heart—a storm of heavenly origin. I was beginning to realize that even though I was professing Christ and the spiritual freedom I had found in Him, I was actually subject to a form of slavery by my entanglements in the entertainment industry. And a storm of rebellion arose in my heart.

How much can I do for Christ here in the belly of the beast? I began asking myself. I started noticing the dark side of the entertainment industry. It was becoming obvious to me that although the dark empire would allow us to speak of Christ, it was willing to let us go only so far. To act like a Christian was fine, to talk like a Christian was fine, to make music about Christ was fine, but when we attempted to live out the principles of the gospel in our lives, we had crossed a line.

One night we were in the studio recording a song when our producer commented, "You know, the label thinks you guys are getting a little bit too preachy." As he was speaking, it was as though I heard the Lord saying to me, *"Soon your career as a hip-hop artist will be over."* "That's too bad," I replied. "This is the message the Lord has given us, and nothing will change that." That ended the conversation. But I understood now that the empire of darkness would allow us to go only so far in proclaiming the message of the pure gospel.

The Riders of the Storm were now all *in* the storm. We knew that God was leading us. The question was: Where was He leading? Were we to ride the storm deeper into the darkness of the entertainment industry? Or was God leading us to ride the storm out of it?

One morning Vex told me of a dream he had had the night before. In it, he said, there was an explosion. Rising out of the flames were the four us, unscathed, each raising one hand in the air tightly clenching a microphone. *What an impressive dream,* I thought. Vex thought it meant that we would persevere through the fires of worldliness to do a great work for God as rappers. But from that moment, I felt the Lord was going to do what I was beginning to fear He would do. He was going to take us out of the black hole. But microphone in hand . . . ? What did that mean?

I would have to wait to find out.

The Boogie Monsters in a Los Angeles radio station with hip-hop artist PMD. 1994.

10
STAR-WAR REVELATIONS

Uneasiness followed me at every turn. I had become deeply concerned over our present work for God. Was it really for Him? Was He leading us or not? Was I doing His will or mine? So many people had personally told us about the positive effect our music was having on them. *How could He not be using us?*

I wasn't the only one struggling. As we made our way to downtown Manhattan on the train one morning, Sean said, "Guys, I've been doing some studying, and I think we need to take the drums out of our music."

Silence. We looked at him as if he were from Neptune.

"I think the drums—the way we use them—might not be right. I've been reading that the way drums are played can have a negative effect on people. I'm not sure how, but I believe it."

Silence. We stared at him, trying to absorb this bizarre idea!

Finally, one of us broke in, "No drums? No *drums?* Are you crazy? Drums are the lifeblood of our music. Without drums we can't move the crowd!" I remember thinking,

Why in the world would we want to get rid of the hypnotic beat?

Sean continued undaunted, "Another thing—I think we need to stop boasting about ourselves and our skills when we rhyme."

Now we were thinking, *Pluto. He must be from Pluto.*

"That's far out, Sean, really far out."

We argued all the way to the studio. Sean was obviously struggling with these convictions. The Lord had been speaking to him. Even though we didn't have much understanding of God's ways, we felt He was using us. I remember one young woman we met in Canada about this time. She was white but had taken up the Rastafarian culture. She asked to come to our hotel room after the performance, intent on getting high with us. We invited her to our room, but to her surprise, we opened the Word of God! It had an intense effect on her. After our study together, she talked about how impressed she was that we were trying to live the message we were preaching.

Over the next several months, the battle continued to rage within me. *Am I in God's will or not?* I decided to turn to His Word for answers—and I was astonished by what I found. I was an avid reader of the book of Revelation and came across these words:

> There appeared another wonder in heaven; and behold a great red dragon, having seven heads and ten horns, and seven crowns upon his heads. And his tail drew the third part of the stars of heaven, and did cast them to the earth (Revelation 12:3, 4).

I learned that the "stars" mentioned here were not literal rocky objects in space but a symbol of angels. Verse 9 went on to say, "And the great dragon was cast out, that old serpent, called the Devil, and Satan, which deceiveth the whole world: he was cast out into the earth, *and his angels were cast out with him*" (emphasis added).

Then the Lord put this question into my heart: *"Why were these 'stars' cast out of heaven?"* Then I thought of Isaiah 14:12.

How art thou fallen from heaven, O Lucifer, son of the morning! How art thou cut down to the ground, which didst weaken the nations! For thou hast said in thine heart, I will ascend into heaven, I will exalt my throne above the stars of God: I will sit also upon the mount of the congregation, in the sides of the north: I will ascend above the heights of the clouds; I will be like the most High.

The Bible says that Lucifer, as one of the "stars" of God, was cast out of heaven because he wanted to exalt himself above God. Suddenly it dawned on me that Lucifer (light bearer) lost his position in heaven because he wanted to be *more famous than God!* Then God prodded me with a further question: *"Where does the desire to be exalted above others come from?"* I had to admit that it originated with Lucifer. It was his pride that caused his fall. The Greek word *huperephanos* (pride) means literally "to appear above others." Lucifer fell because he wanted to outshine God Himself (see Ezekiel 28:17). When I compared the desire for fame with Christ's character, I saw they were total opposites. The Bible describes Christ like this: "Let this mind be in you, which was also in Christ Jesus: Who, being in the form of God, thought it not robbery to be equal with God: *But made him-*

self of no reputation, and took upon him the form of a servant, and was made *in the likeness of men:* And being found in fashion as a man, *he humbled himself*, and became obedient unto death, even the death of the cross" (Philippians 2:5–8, emphasis supplied).

I was beginning to see that the principle of the Cross was the opposite of exaltation. And I knew that my career was based on self-exaltation. Pride was the center of this whole entertainment industry, this black hole. Pride meant that The Boogie Monsters had to walk and talk a certain way. The carnal nature of our audience demanded that we reflect some form of pride. In fact, without pride, it would be impossible to advance in the industry. I knew that I could never be humble onstage. I began to compare the album covers of professed Christian hip-hop artists with those of secular rap groups—and noticed the same look of pride and sensuality. Who was being promoted on these covers—Christ or the artist? Was the audience coming to our concerts to hear a word from Christ or from us? As I reflected on all this, I realized that the soul of the entertainment industry consisted in trying to outperform the competition. The lifeblood of the black hole was the very same need that Lucifer had exhibited in trying to exalt himself above his fellow angels and above God.

Then it struck me that once these fallen stars were cast out of heaven, they went to work to seduce human beings into the same course, using the same principle of self-exaltation. The Lord quietly prodded me again: *What are people called who exalt themselves above others in the entertainment industry?* Stars! They call themselves stars! Suddenly the star war took on a whole new dimension. Human stars were being used by fallen angelic stars to turn people's minds from the Bright and Morning Star, Jesus Christ. Whether they realized it or not, these human stars were actually star warriors of the dark side—and I was one of them!

The Spirit had more to say: *"And where is the home of these fallen stars now? Where is their headquarters, the city of these fallen angels?"* The answer hit me like a brick—*Hollywood.* The home of the stars, the city of lost angels, was Hollywood and Los Angeles, whose very name means the "city of angels." This was the center of the black hole, the capital of the dark empire, the city of the lost angels! Like no other power, the entertainment industry was responsible for drawing humanity away from submitting to the laws of God's heavenly kingdom.

These discoveries made it increasingly difficult for me to believe that I was doing God's will. But I kept my convictions to myself. I tried to find reasons why I was not like other stars; I tried to convince myself that I *could* be humble. I told myself that although my style of dress didn't lend itself to the principles of humility, I could nonetheless reveal humility when I spoke. I was sure that somewhere the Bible says that God doesn't care about the way we dress. *Where is that text?* But even my spoken humility would have to be limited to what I said in interviews; a rap star can *never* rhyme in humility. *He must show his skills.* When entertaining, humility must go out the window.

So, under the guise of a love for God, I challenged the devil—as if I had some power within me to stand up to him. Today, I wince as I hear Christian hip-hop artists boastfully claiming to "smack" the devil. It reminds me of the story found in Acts 19:13–16:

> Then certain of the vagabond Jews, exorcists, took upon them to call over them which had evil spirits the

name of the Lord Jesus, saying, We adjure you by Jesus whom Paul preacheth. And there were seven sons of one Sceva, a Jew, and chief of the priests, which did so. And the evil spirit answered and said, Jesus I know, and Paul I know; but who are ye? And the man in whom the evil spirit was leaped on them, and overcame them, and prevailed against them, so that they fled out of that house naked and wounded.

If any of The Boogie Monsters would have had a face-to-face meeting with the powers of darkness, we, too, would have found all our chanting "in the name of Jesus" to be useless. Even though these men used Jesus' name, they didn't have Jesus' power. Nor did we.

Another story in the book of Acts also has something to say about the principles that lead to so-called Christian rap music or rock and roll. Luke, who was traveling with the apostle Paul, says:

And it came to pass, as we went to prayer, a certain damsel possessed with a spirit of divination met us, which brought her masters much gain by soothsaying: The same followed Paul and us, and cried, saying, These men are the servants of the most high God, which shew unto us the way of salvation. And this did she many days. But Paul, being grieved, turned and said to the spirit, I command thee in the name of Jesus Christ to come out of her. And he came out the same hour (Acts 16:16–18).

The woman possessed with an evil spirit did something very unlikely. Notice that her words were inspired words of truth! Why would the evil spirits inspire her to speak words of truth? The answer is simple. The people of the town knew this woman to be involved in divination. Without the evidence of a changed life, as long as she continued her connection with the evil spirits, her words were a mockery of God. And so, Paul, a skilled light warrior, rebuked the evil spirits.

Without question, the hip-hop and rock cultures are opposed to God's values. The music is an inseparable part of the sinful culture of contemporary society. When music groups try to use Christian words of truth while still clinging to the culture of hip-hop and rock, they are engaged in a mockery of God. Pop culture and its music causes division even in worldly circles. I have seen and experienced it first-hand. So, it should come as no surprise that when these things are brought into the church, disguised as "sanctified," they continue to cause serious divisions and bitter feelings between brothers and sisters in Christ.

The truth is that without a living connection with Christ that produces a fruitful life, our words are of no value, even if they are words of truth. If we do not understand what it means to come out of the world and its ways, we are in constant danger of making a mockery of God and the Christian faith.

11
THE DARK SIDE UNVEILED

For some time I remained silent about the struggle going on within me. One of the issues that worried me was my future: *What will I do if I give up this eight-album contract?* I had dropped out of Virginia State University. I had no intention of ever going back to college. Surprisingly, my parents were now encouraging our newfound fame. As far as the world could see, all was going well. How could I explain to my parents what the Lord had been impressing on me? They already thought Sean and I were crazy for becoming Seventh-day Adventists. And how could I share my convictions with the other members of the group without offending them? What would my own brother say?

Meanwhile, I continued to witness. The video shoot of one of our songs called for a large cast. As we pulled these people together, I ran across some artists who began discussing the new world order and its accompanying conspiracy theories. They began talking about the mark of the beast and how the world would end. I shared with them what the Scriptures had to say on the matter. They were silent and awestruck. More and more, my heart was moved to do the

Lord's work and tell people about the good news of Jesus Christ and His truth. It was all I could think about.

My Bible studies continued to consume me to the point that I was now studying before and after concerts. I bought notepads and scribbled thoughts and meditations while on trains, planes, and automobiles. The more I opened my mind to the influence of God's Word, the more these thoughts seemed to flow through me like a refreshing stream—and the more I was able to think clearly about my situation.

I began searching the Scriptures even more intensely, seeking answers to my dilemma. The Lord was opening my mind to the black hole that I was in. As an artist, I always tried to see things and express things in a unique way, and this is how God chose to appeal to me. He allowed me to see His truths in a unique and compelling way.

For example, as I read the story of the demoniac in Mark 5, I learned that two signs of demonic possession were naked-ness and a "wrong mind." After Jesus cast out the demons from this man, the people saw the former demoniac "sitting, and clothed, and in his right mind: and they were afraid" (verse 15). I learned that this was also the state in which Adam and Eve were in when they sinned and listened to Satan's lies—they were naked and confused. Satan had drawn them into his black hole. After their sin, they realized that they were naked and in their wrong minds. They were fearful of a loving and seeking Savior (see Genesis 3:5–8). In fact, Satan used a form of hypnosis, or mind control, over the pair. And it was through a medium, the serpent, that Satan was able to hypnotize them. And then it hit me that Satan was likewise using a medium today—the modern mass me-dia—the plural of the word medium—to hypnotize millions of people. I knew that in itself the media was not evil, but I also knew that Satan was using it for his purposes.

And now I was seeing that music, too, could possess a deadly hypnotic influence. Recent rock idol Kurt Cobain incited a music revolution and then committed suicide. The 1992 release of the classic and deadly video for the song "Jeremy" by Pearl Jam seemed innocent art. But it was to become an ominous sign of a new and deadly trend in school violence. One reporter described the 1999 Columbine tragedy with these words:

> As I've watched and read the reports of what took place at Columbine High School last Tuesday—events that were, at the same time, sickening, incomprehensible and obscenely riveting—time and time again words and images from Pearl Jam's rock video, *Jeremy*, have come into my mind. . . . Pearl Jam's video, made in 1992, tells the true story of a boy who, in the ominous, oft-repeated words of the song, *spoke in class today*. Jeremy is a disturbed and unhappy child. Daddy doesn't pay attention. Mommy only cares about her clothes. Classmates ridicule him. And the serpent, which is subtler than all the other creatures, finds an opportunity. Jeremy spoke in class today. He speaks through violence. Striding into school after the lesson has already begun, he blows his brains out before his tormentors. Try to forget this, try to erase this from the blackboard, he sneers. . . . Jeremy spoke in class today. So too did Eric and Dylan. But there is no question, too, that they spoke with the instantly recognizable, cynical and contemptuous accents of popular culture—the Hollywood movies,

TV shows and computer games that fed their imaginations and molded their mental landscapes. Eat this, sucker. Hasta la vista, baby. See this and die (*Ship of Fools*, April 1999).

Other key words would soon come alive with meaning about the black hole of the entertainment industry. Take *television*, for example. *Tele* means to communicate at a distance, and *vision* refers to sight. I would soon understand that one of Satan's most effective methods of communicating his characteristics to humans is through television. Studies have revealed that the very images on the screen can produce an effect that is potentially hypnotic and dangerous, introducing impressions into the subconscious mind to effect action or change. I began to realize that kids who were watching the popular shows like *Beverly Hills, 90210* were hypnotically affected. They were acting out what they had seen on the screen, subconsciously doing what was contrary to God's Word and His will. Young girls who watched what these divas were wearing would go out and buy the same clothes. Today, I watch young kids from every walk of life reveal the fatal fact that they are a hypnotized generation. The 2004 movie remake of the '70s hit series *Starsky and Hutch*, for example, sent many of my peers into a '70s fad frenzy!

Then there is the word *channel*, usually thought of as the dial that controls the TV stations we want to watch. But the word can also refer to another of Satan's effective methods of snaring the multitudes. *Channeling* is the method through which many New Agers and spiritualists communicate with evil spirits. So, too, when people sit down before the television set and view various channels through which Satan works, they are opening themselves up to evil spirits, experiencing a one-way communication with them, and transferring the evil being portrayed on the screen into their minds. In this way, millions of people are being sucked into the black hole through pornography, violence, and a godless value system.

Consider the word *amuse.* If Christians realized that the definition of this word is "to divert from serious business" or that its primary meaning is to "deceive or cheat by first occupying the attention," perhaps they would be more apt to discern that Satan is playing a deadly game for their souls. He is deceiving young people by diverting them with thousands of amusements, cheating them out of eternal life while firmly occupying their attention.

And then I thought about the word *programming.* Yes, millions are being programmed by what they listen to and view. I had been programmed extensively by all these cultural media, but the Lord wanted to reprogram me. He wanted to pull me out of this entertainment industry that causes so much confusion. And then finally God's message hit me! I had wondered why our group's "ministry" was not having the effect I thought it should have had. We would tell our audiences to "give it up for Jesus," and they would go wild "for Jesus" with forty-ounce beer bottles and marijuana blunts in their hands. It was becoming crystal clear to me—I could not call people out of the black hole if I was still in the black hole myself!

At this time, neither my appearance nor my slang language gave any hint that I was a Christian. Appearance meant nothing to me. I took pride in my incognito "Christian" appearance. I liked to see people staring at my dreadlocks and rugged clothing. I reveled in the potential shock factor whenever someone discovered that I was a Christian who avidly studied the Bible!

But as God continued to speak to me and I tried to imagine Jesus on the stage rapping—in humility—I began to realize it could not be done. As a rap artist, it was my nature to perform in pride in front of screaming fans. Even when I turned to Christian hip-hop and started rhyming about humility, I soon learned that it was impossible to reflect true humility in a culture in which self is the center. According to Scripture, light and darkness cannot mix, and I knew it. Light was calling me out of the black hole.

12

A BEHIND "THE SEEN" LOOK AT THE DARK EMPIRE

As I look back, I am amazed at the effect the black hole of the entertainment industry had on me. Many people are unaware of what is behind that industry. To get a good view of what is behind the *scene*, I have learned that one must first look behind the "seen"! As the scripture says, "We wrestle not against flesh and blood, but against principalities, against powers, against the rulers of the darkness of this world, against spiritual wickedness in high places" (Ephesians 6:12).

It especially is troubling to me today to see the effect the entertainment industry is having on my peers in the church. Parents are at a loss to know what to do. Some seem to be unaware of the supernatural forces involved. The black hole is engulfing so many kids, so many young adults. They are being drawn into it as if pulled by some gigantic magnet, and they seem powerless to break the fatal attraction. Hollywood's stars are being used by Satan's unseen "stars" to successfully recruit millions to become devoted students of the dark side. Even worse, the black hole seems to be making its way into the church itself! As I travel to many different churches, I hear the same thing from many concerned parents and youth—the entertainment industry is having a devastating effect on the church. Many know more about violent and sexual video games, the hottest music, and the latest fads in dress and movies than they do about the Bible.

This black hole saps spiritual desire and energy, leaving its victims unresponsive to spiritual life. It is like a deadly drug that holds its subjects captive and craving more and more. And especially troubling is the fact that the hypnotic power exercised by Satan through the media is not noticed by those who are most enthralled by it. Many are being "remote controlled." The media puts a hilarious and harmless spin on this whole hypnotic experience, but the Bible reveals that those who are caught up in it are under the control of the mind of Satan. The apostle Paul calls it "the snare of the devil" and being "taken captive by him at his will" (2 Timothy 2:26).

When Adam and Eve sinned, they fell under Satan's hypnotic power. Before Eve opened herself up to the voice of the tempter, she understood with clarity what God had said; He had instructed the first pair about right and wrong. Her spiritual sight was clear. When she looked at the tree, she knew it was evil to eat from it and that its fruit could result only in death. But the Bible says that after Satan spoke, "The woman saw that the *tree was good for food*, and that it was *pleasant to the eyes*, and a tree *to be desired* to make one wise, she took of the fruit thereof, and did eat, and gave also unto her husband with her; and he did eat" (Genesis 3:6, emphasis supplied).

When disobedience ceased to look sinful and appeared desirable instead, this was the result of Satan's hypnosis.

And the very same thing is occurring today. The fallen "stars," Satan's angels, are using the media to hypnotize thousands of youth and young adults. The media uses captivating movies to engender a craving for more and more of Satan's mind control. Consider the words the media uses to promote upcoming movies: *drama, mystery, action, explosive, sizzling, sensational, seductive, passionate.* When it's time to go to church, and there are no explosive, action-packed pictures in front of them, the youth become bored, lose interest, or fall asleep. So, to keep the youth awake and interested, the church may be tempted to use the very same techniques of Hollywood.

The Harry Potter phenomenon is sweeping the hearts of kids all across the world. This subtle teaching of witchcraft under the guise of harmless entertainment is doing great harm. The Bible warns against witchcraft because it involves communion with demonic "stars" or angels:

> There shall not be found among you any one that maketh his son or his daughter to pass through the fire, or that useth divination, or an observer of times, or an enchanter, *or a witch*, or a charmer, or a consulter with familiar spirits, or a wizard, or a necromancer. For all that do these things are an abomination unto the LORD: and because of these abominations the LORD thy God doth drive them out from before thee (Deuteronomy 18:10–12, emphasis supplied).

The Bible lists witchcraft as one of the works of the flesh. "Now the works of the flesh are manifest, which are these; adultery, fornication, uncleanness, lasciviousness, idolatry, witchcraft, hatred, variance, emulations, wrath, strife, seditions, heresies" (Galatians 5:19, 20). When witchcraft is made to look attractive and seemingly harmless, young people are tempted to become involved.

However, the insidious nature of witchcraft goes much deeper than most people realize. When people think about sorcery and witchcraft, they usually associate them with Harry Potter, voodoo, Ouija boards, and psychics. Certainly these things are part of what witchcraft and sorcery are all about. However, the Bible warns that sorcery will play a major role in deceiving the world in the last days (see Revelation 18:23). The Greek word used for sorcery is *pharmakeia,* meaning "to medicate." Our English words *pharmacy* and *pharmaceuticals* are derived from this word. Thus, the Bible is saying that anything that medicates the mind so it turns from God is sorcery. Paul confirms this when he writes, "O foolish Galatians, who hath bewitched you, that ye should not obey the truth" (Galatians 3:1).

When we think of such drugs as cocaine and marijuana, we realize that they indeed medicate the mind so it cannot follow the will of God. Alcohol, also known as "spirits," does precisely the same thing. These habits are so hard to break because they involve warfare with unseen supernatural powers. But is it possible that television, contemporary music, and the entertainment industry also medicate the mind, effectively crippling its spiritual powers? The answer is obvious. Behind *the seen* we are dealing with evil supernatural powers. This is why young and old alike are powerless to break the spell. Human power alone cannot break the power of supernatural sorcery. Human intellect alone cannot detect or discern what lies behind *the seen*. Without the wisdom and armor of God, we are as lambs brought to the slaughter.

The Bible compares rebellion with witchcraft. "For rebellion is as the sin of witchcraft, and stubbornness is as iniquity and idolatry" (1 Samuel 15:23). Anything that fosters the spirit of rebellion is strengthening Satan's powers of witchcraft and sorcery over the mind. Most teens think that they are simply watching *Buffy the Vampire Slayer* or reading Harry Potter books; that they are not engulfed by the phenomena; that they are unaffected by witchcraft and sorcery. This is one of the great deceptions of the dark side.

Ellen White once described the power of spiritualism as being like a train on which the whole world seemed to be on board. Satan, the engineer, was guiding the train with lightning speed to perdition while the passengers were unaware of their danger. As I think about the title of the popular television music program *Soul Train*, I can't help thinking of Satan's mocking message to an ignorant world, unaware that it is being assaulted by spiritualism through the media. The world, as well as many Christians, is dancing to the deadly rhythm of the enemy of souls. The "soul train" is fast filling up with passengers who do not understand its final destination. And music is one of the main attractions used to draw people on board.

Consider the roots of this musical component of the black hole. In the rocking '50s and '60s, music became the main weapon of rebellion. It hypnotized an entire generation. For almost two thousand years "rock" music was music about the Rock—Jesus Christ. But in one decade, a new "rock" would emerge, encouraging the young to rebel against God's principles. The volatile '60s, ignited by rebellion against the war in Vietnam, soon sparked rebellion in every other area of life. In its wake, sex, drugs, and rock and roll became the mantra for thousands of young adults all over America.

Television, though moving at a much slower pace, would soon become the next weapon of Satan's revolution. It began with programs such as *Leave it to Beaver* and other family friendly shows. But as music began to hypnotize the young, television began to reflect this change in society. The downward progression of television programming has come to the place that today society views such programs as *Queer Eye for the Straight Guy* and other aberrant, antifamily oriented shows as "normal."

The Bible clearly warns that astrology, the study of the stars to determine one's future, is evil:

> Stand now with thine enchantments, and with the multitude of thy sorceries, wherein thou hast laboured from thy youth; if so be thou shalt be able to profit, if so be thou mayest prevail. Thou art wearied in the multitude of thy counsels. Let now the astrologers, the stargazers, the monthly prognosticators, stand up, and save thee from these things that shall come upon thee. Behold, they shall be as stubble; the fire shall burn them; they shall not deliver themselves from the power of the flame (Isaiah 47:12–14).

But could it be that Satan has created a new wave of astrology through the stars of the entertainment industry? The truth is that although most people do not study the stars in the sky to determine their future, they are stargazers, nonetheless—studying carefully the stars in Hollywood for clues as to how to live their own lives. From what to wear to their aspirations and behavior, many of these modern stargazers

are ignorantly involved in Satan's most subtle and dangerous form of astrology.

In reality, there is only one escape from the black hole,
only one door, one avenue, through which a person can
elude this powerful magnetic pull that draws its victims ever
downward. That one door is Jesus Christ. A full surrender to
Him is our only safety. In this world of darkness, the only
ones who escape are those who follow the triumphant Rebel
against darkness! Jesus Christ, the Light of this world, re-
belled against every principle of darkness and submitted to
none of the ways of wickedness. When the believers in
Corinth, once steeped in sorcery and witchcraft, gave themselves over to God, it is recorded that "many of them also
which used curious arts brought their books together, and
burned them before all men" (Acts 19:19). Once we cove-
nant with God to fight the attraction of the black hole in the
strength of the Mighty Conqueror, Jesus, there will be
invisible armies of light to assist us, and they will break
the power of hypnosis over us. The armies of heaven rejoice
when those who were once rebels against light become rebels against darkness. Once we surrender our wills to Christ,
He empowers us, making us rebels against darkness. In sur-
rendering all, we forsake every weapon of the enemy—his
drugs, his CDs, his programming, his alcohol, his partying,
all of it. Satan's hypnotic power will end their dominion in
our lives as we break, destroy, and burn those weapons he
has used to control us. We will end Satan's hypnotic dominion over our lives. Like the early Corinthian Christians, we,
too, must destroy those things that give Satan access to our
minds.

I think of my good friend Phillip, once in the black hole,
who has by God's grace escaped and is now a "star warrior,"

a pastor in New York. Then there is Marquis, once a comrade rebel against light, poised for a major recording contract, now a fellow rebel against the empire of darkness and an evangelist for God. And there are many others who even now are set to be snatched from the dark side. By God's grace, they will rise against the powers of rebellion and have their eyes opened to see—behind *the seen*—the principalities and powers of wickedness at work deceiving souls. The good news is that God is raising up an army. He is snatching soldiers of darkness from the dark empire and making them soldiers of light, warriors of brightness. While the soul train is making its way to perdition, there is another soul train with Christ at its head. He is calling us to come on board, to change our destinations, and let Him free us from the power of the enemy.

He has done this for me and desires to do it for all who are enslaved in the black hole!

13

Drawn From the Dark Side

I will never forget the 1956 movie thriller *Invasion of the Body Snatchers*. Of course, I was not even born when it was released, but I watched it in the '80s—and afterward, I thought about never going to sleep again! The movie depicts an invasion of aliens who take over the bodies of thousands who do nothing more than go to sleep. These aliens look like the real person they have invaded but reveal no emotion whatever. Humans who realize what is going on have to begin acting emotionless, as well, or they will be discovered, pointed out, and hunted down by the aliens. For the humans, the counterfeits are hard to spot, except that they have no emotions. Discovering that a loved one is no longer human, but an alien, is bone-chilling.

In a way, my journey out of the black hole was similar to this movie. Instead of people, it was the things that I had once loved that began to appear alien, hideous underneath, void of any godly virtue. Indeed these things were hard to spot until the Lord began to shed light on my mind. I had been as one asleep to these dangers, but now the Lord was waking me up.

Television, to which I had been addicted, began to reveal some very ugly things. Not that it hadn't always been so, but my eyes were now being opened and made sensitive to the Spirit of God and the spirit of sin. I began to notice that many of the programs I loved were actually alien to God's kingdom of righteousness and peace. Violence, cursing, and sexuality seemed to pervade every TV show. I soon found it unbearable to watch television while I was striving for holiness in Christ.

Likewise, the movie theater that I once loved to attend became a hideous thing that was encouraging thousands to unwittingly commit sin in their hearts. Whether it was cheering for the hero who had just "blown away" the bad guy, enjoying the scenes of adultery, or mentally engaging in the love scenes, I found the movie theater had become a place for sins of the heart. So I stopped going to movies—until I heard about a movie that was dealing with the book of Revelation. Eagerly, I went to the theater, thinking that here, at last, would be something worth watching. By the first quarter of the movie I was disgusted. The plot revolved around a supposedly hidden book in Revelation—a twenty-third chapter. In this chapter, Gabriel becomes an evil angel. Satan destroys him, claiming, "There can be only one devil in town!" I walked out of the theater after thirty minutes, sick to my stomach. It was my last time in a movie theater.

As a child, I enjoyed nothing more than watching Saturday morning cartoon marathons. Now I began to see why Satan had orchestrated Saturday as "cartoon morning." Millions of kids, captivated by the television screen, would find keeping the Sabbath a terrible burden.

Also, these cartoons always seemed to teach mixed principles and values—and, surprisingly, spiritualism. Over the past seven decades, Disney has released film after film containing covert or overt spiritualism. *Pinocchio*—a talking piece of wood—originates from Celtic and Nordic myths of talking trees. *Snow White and the Seven Dwarfs* introduced children to "good witches" and lovable dwarfs who are magical little beings like elves. *Fantasia, Cinderella, Alice in Wonderland, Peter Pan, Sleeping Beauty, The Sword in the Stone, The Little Mermaid, Beauty and the Beast, Aladdin, Hercules, Arabian Nights, Atlantis: The Lost Empire, and Toy Story* all are mingled with magic, sorcery, and ancient mystical teachings. Walt Disney's Magic Kingdom is the largest producer of spiritualistic films in the world. Over the last decade or so a new class of cartoons has been produced that caters to a much older audience. From *Ren and Stimpy* to *The Simpsons* to *South Park*, cartoons became more violent and debased. Realizing that almost nothing positive or productive was coming out of the television screen, I cut it out of my life.

And then there was the whole area of martial arts, which I had loved from childhood. In mimicking the five animals—dragon, snake, crane, tiger, and leopard—and trying to take on their "spirits," I had no clue that I had been inviting the spirit of demons into my life. The entire system of martial arts is closely intertwined with spiritualism. I began to realize this as more and more kung fu movies included contact with the dead and martial artists who possessed supernatural powers. In one such movie, the spirit of a dying ninja takes possession of an innocent woman, and she becomes a deadly ninja warrior. The recent hit *Crouching Tiger, Hidden Dragon* combines spiritualism with the martial arts in a way that has swept many young people deeper into the black hole.

I soon learned that the martial arts are a counterfeit of the true fighting art of faith. When God came to Cain, who was struggling with ill feelings toward his brother, He encouraged Cain to resist sin:

> And the LORD said unto Cain, Why art thou wroth? and why is thy countenance fallen? If thou doest well, shalt thou not be accepted? and if thou doest not well, sin lieth at the door. And unto thee shall be his desire, and thou shalt rule over him (Genesis 4:6, 7).

It is interesting to note that the Hebrew word for "rule" is *mashawl*, meaning "to dominate" or "to master." It is very similar to our English word *martial*, which means "warlike," hence the "martial" arts. In fact, in Roman mythology Mars was the god of war. When God told Cain to *mashawl* against sin, He was encouraging him to be a spiritual martial artist against sin! In the NIV, Genesis 4:6, 7 says it this way:

> Then the LORD said to Cain, "Why are you angry? Why is your face downcast? If you do what is right, will you not be accepted? But if you do not do what is right, sin is *crouching* at your door; it desires to have you, but you must master it" (emphasis added).

Yes, sin was lurking like a crouching tiger and a hidden dragon. When it was released in Cain's life and took possession of his spirit, Cain killed his brother—in typical dragon style under the influence of that old serpent, Satan. Rather than spiritually master his sin as God had commanded, Cain twisted it to physically master his brother.

Once I saw the truth about the hobby I had once cherished, the martial arts suddenly lost their appeal. This, too, was an alien, a foreign creature, that I had believed was normal and harmless. I pulled away, deserted it, and never turned back. The gravitational pull of the black hole was losing its hold on me.

Then there was the hip-hop culture I had grown to love so dearly. Hip-hop was more than just music, you see. It was a way of life penetrating one's soul. One had to walk and talk a certain way and wear certain styles of clothing. This, too, began to reveal its ugly nature. I tried to picture Christ doing these things, but the Word of God was too clear:

> But I say, that the things which the Gentiles sacrifice, they sacrifice to devils, and not to God: and I would not that ye should have fellowship with devils. Ye cannot drink the cup of the Lord, and the cup of devils: ye cannot be partakers of the Lord's table, and of the table of devils (1 Corinthians 10:20, 21).

In looking like the world, talking like the world, and dressing like the world, I had identified myself with the world. Although Christ became one of us and took on our humanity, He was careful not to cater to individual or national pride. Because He refused to take on the national pride that Israel had assumed, His own rejected Him (see John 1:11). The hip-hop culture caters to black pride, while its style of dress caters to human pride. Christ also rejected anything that was not holy and respectable. He did not speak the slang of the day. His words were pure, untainted, and always holy. Because of this, I began to see that beneath the hip-hop culture was an alien spirit whose intent was to draw me away from the humility of Christ.

Eventually the club scene, which I had so relished, began to reveal its ugly side. One night after a performance in Philadelphia, we went down into the crowd to hang out and mingle with the people. I had given up drinking and marijuana by this time; so, I know I was not high. But as I walked through the people dancing on the floor, the party suddenly turned fearful. It suddenly *seemed* to me that the people were controlled by evil spirits who were moving their bodies in the heat of sensuality. In my mind's eye I saw spirits riding the bodies of the people. I was fast losing my desire for everything I had once loved. I was in a world of many deceptions, and I felt as though I was the only one who could see their hideous reality and true origins. With each new discovery, I felt like another load was being lifted from me in my struggle to draw closer to God. I felt lightness in my soul. The gravitational pull of the black hole was losing its force, and I was being pulled out of the dark empire.

14
ESCAPE FROM THE BLACK HOLE

Crossroads. That is the one word that comes to mind as I think of that night in Queens, New York, with the four of us standing on the steps of my aunt Fay's house. Only months earlier we had been introduced to the Bible in a powerful way. We had plans to take this gospel to the world through our music. But God had plans, as well, and now we were at the crossroads.

The storm we were so eager to ride when we left college, the winds of fame we were so eager to fly upon, had taken an unexpected turn—from secular rap group to Adventism to Christian rap group, and now this crossroad. An incredible struggle was going on in my soul. Was I walking in the light of the Lord, or was I following my own will? I soon discovered that my brother Sean was also struggling inside his own heart with the same issues.

Our second contract term was coming up, and we knew that time was of the essence. The scenario presented itself to me over and over: hip-hop stars, standing for Jesus, leading a mass exodus out of darkness into light through their music. But that picture was at war with another scene in my mind. I had become keenly aware of the invisible star war going on in the universe and in each heart. The dark empire with its capital, the black hole, had been revealed.

For me, the lights and glamour of the entertainment industry were fast losing their luster. The scene from Matthew's Gospel where Christ is in the wilderness being tempted of the devil loomed before me. The words presented themselves to me in great significance: "Again, the devil taketh him [Jesus] up into an exceeding high mountain, and sheweth him all the kingdoms of the world, and the glory of them; and saith unto him, All these things will I give thee, if thou wilt fall down and worship me" (Matthew 4:8, 9). The Boogie Monsters could win the world, we could accomplish our gospel mission with hip-hop, but the price was compromise—compromise with the fashions and principles of the dark empire, compromise of the Sabbath, compromise by fellowshiping with the works of darkness.

This picture settled it for me. We had moved to Virginia during the summer of 1995, and I had plenty of time to think. Another obstacle presented itself to me. We had signed an eight-album contract. How could I legally get out of this commitment without any repercussions? Falling to my knees one night, in the quietness of our Virginia home, I prayed to God, "Lord, I am ready to leave this industry for You. I know that many will not understand, but I understand. Lord, please, if You take me from behind this microphone, put me behind another that I still may be able to reach the world with this message." I felt as though the Lord replied, "I will bring you again before many." I made my decision to abandon the dark side and follow the Lamb wherever He would lead me.

Now it was time to break the news to my brother. In solemn tones we talked. "Sean, I've made my decision."

Silence. Then he replied, "Me, too."

I was surprised. "I can't go on," I told him.

"Me either," he answered.

My brother, independent of my decision, had come to the same conclusion at the same time! Suddenly, the great load that I had been bearing rolled off my back. The gravitational pull of the black hole suddenly lost its power over me. *I was free!* The scary thing was that until that moment I had never realized that I had been so totally trapped in its power. My brother and I were together on this, as we had so often been on so many major events in our lives. That night, "Yoda" and "Jedi" were laid to rest.

But we still had the problem of how to get out of our eight-album contract. Sean and I began to pray for a way out. It wasn't long until we got a phone call from our manager telling us the "bad" news that our label, Pendulum/EMI, had folded! We were not certain how this happened, but we saw it as a Godsend! God shut down an entire record label to release us from our contract! He had opened the sea before us and provided us a way of escape.

I had felt His invitation already—calling me to leave the world behind and enter a new "star war." Now this invitation seemed to be calling me to go deeper, further away than I had expected. I had no idea where this new star war would lead me nor how I would be able to affect anyone in the backwoods of Virginia.

Now here we were, at the crossroads. We met up in New York, the four of us—Mondo, Vex, Sean, and myself—riders of a storm that was about to scatter us in different directions. Our future was uncertain, but we knew why we had gathered. All along we had talked about the issues, but now it was time for one side to convince the other. Mondo and

Vex felt as though they were doing God's will through the music. Another label had offered to pick us up, but Sean and I decided that we would not continue.

"So," I began, "Sean and I have decided that we are not going to continue with the group. God has convicted us that this is not what He wants for us."

"That's cool," Mondo replied.

"Yeah, the way I see it, God has shown us that this is His will for us, and He has called us to spread God's message through our music," Vex added.

"Babylon won't allow you to speak the truth," Sean countered. "God is calling us to something higher."

"Who is gonna reach the hip-hop generation but us? God has called you to this, Yoda!" Vex exclaimed.

I momentarily felt the faint pulling of the force that had once dominated me. But a new power had taken control of my life. "Vex, my conscience will no longer allow me to walk in both light and darkness."

The four of us knew that this was it. Sean and I wanted Vex and Mondo to cross that Red Sea with us. They wanted us to stay with them in Egypt to battle the forces of evil. Both sides were fully convinced in their own minds. We knew there was not much more to be said. Both sides sensed the other could not be persuaded.

"Do you honestly think you'll be able to spread an undiluted message through a secular avenue?" I asked them both.

"No doubt," they replied.

I felt a sense of helplessness as I saw we were getting nowhere. This was where we would part. "What do you want us to tell people when they ask about you?" Vex and Mondo wanted to know.

"Tell them that we gave this up for Christ," I said.

We lingered for a few more moments, reassuring one another that we were still friends to the end. I thought about Vex's dream—the one of an explosion and us rising out of it with microphones in our hands. One thing was certain, the explosion was happening now, and it was separating Sean and me from Vex and Mondo. But why did all four of us have microphones in the dream? Surely, Sean and I had no plans to start our own rap group.

Before we parted we offered up our last prayer together. It was much different from the one we had first prayed on our opening night performance. The line, "Lead us not into temptation, but deliver us from evil," had been fulfilled in a way we had not expected. Then, we had prayed for the audience. Now, we prayed for one another. It was our last prayer together as The Boogie Monsters. That day, Sean and I—Jedi and Yoda—died to the old life. The last stronghold over us had been broken. We were now ex-star warriors of a dark empire, ex-men of the world, riders of a new storm, one between good and evil. We had escaped the overwhelming force of the black hole!

We had yet one more battle ahead of us. Our parents had been adjusting easily to our newfound fame and success. When we became Christians, they were confused but handled it. Now we had to tell them of our decision to leave the industry we had worked so hard to get into. After all our success, after dropping out of school, we were now giving all this up for the Bible? "A lot of reggae and hip-hop artists talk about God," our parents protested. "Why can't you do that?" We tried to explain, but it was impossible. They just couldn't understand.

But I was at peace; the confusion over whether I was pleasing God had ended. I no longer had to perform for the world. I no longer had to live the image that had identified me from the days of my childhood. Being "hard" was no longer important to me. The latest styles and fashions had lost their grip on me. It was when I cut my dreadlocks that my parents began to suspect that this was more than just a phase I was going through. The slang phrases soon dropped from my lips, and in their place the wonderful words of life came pouring out.

My hardest challenge was to stop listening to hip-hop music altogether. This was indeed a tremendous hurdle. But I quickly realized that I could not hold on to the fashions, language, or music of hip-hop without eventually being fully drawn back into the black hole of the entertainment industry.

As Sean and I stood at the crossroads that night in New York, we realized that we were going in an opposite direction than our friends who had also been baptized. Many of us began the journey out of the black hole; only a few made a full escape. Out of a group of more than twenty of my friends who were baptized together, Sean and I were the only ones who initially made a decision to cut loose from the industry. We were the only ones who chose to give up all, to break, burn, and destroy all of Satan's weapons and strongholds so we could be free from their influence. The force would eventually draw many of the rest completely back into the dark empire.

15
LIGHT SABERS
AND
STAR WARRIORS

"You're hired!" After a few minutes of instruction, I hung up the phone not sure whether to be excited or sad. My brother and I were back in Virginia with our parents. No longer in the bustling city and no longer living the life of a star for the dark side. All was quiet. What did life have for us now? Our future was uncertain. I had much thinking to do. What would I do with the rest of my life? I had dropped out of Virginia State University to chase my hip-hop dreams. Now I had come to see those dreams as a deadly illusion. God had intervened and delivered me from the black hole, but was I now to be like a shooting star gone out in obscurity?

Uncertain of my future, I decide to apply for a job. A job! The most embarrassing thing for an ex-star is to have a *regular job*. I humbled myself, went into the local Target store, and took an application. Some days later the manager called to tell me the good news that I had been hired—at a pay rate of $5.50 an hour! I had dropped out of college. Now I wondered, *Is this how I will spend the rest of my life? Will I be doomed to working my way up the Target ladder, perhaps making store manager one day? Shall I rejoice because I have a source of income now or weep as I compare what I had just a few months ago?*

One thing was certain, there was no going back. I joined David of old when he said, "I had rather be a doorkeeper in the house of my God, than to dwell in the tents of wickedness" (Psalm 84:10).

Sean found employment doing highway work at $8.00 an hour. While working at Target, I often met old friends from high school. "You're working *here*?" they would exclaim. "What are *you* doing working *here*?"

I gladly took the opportunity to share with them why I had given up my career to follow Jesus. Sean was not so privileged. People would recognize him while driving past his work site on the road, but he couldn't do any explaining! All he could do was wave as they drove by.

I often pondered what God wanted me to do with the rest of my life. As a writer of music, I began to consider that maybe God wanted me to write spiritual poems. I started writing and eventually compiled a book of more than a hundred poems. I called them "poetic sermons" because each one was about a Bible doctrine or teaching. In creative style, I expounded on Bible subjects.

At the time, I didn't realize the significance of calling these poems "sermons." God was preparing me for something of which I had no clue. The fire to share Jesus that was started in my heart only grew with time. With no way to let it out, especially living in what I considered the boonies, I arranged to make a way to let it out. I gathered some old friends from high school and some of my coworkers, including my manager, and was able to convince them to come to my home for a Bible study. With each study I gave, the fire grew stronger.

Part of the reason for this fire to witness was because of certain influences on my life that occurred when I joined the church back in New York. Shortly after the first half of our group of friends had been baptized, we moved from Queens to Brooklyn. There, we began to attend the Kingsboro Seventh-day Adventist Church, where Sean and I were eventually baptized along with the second half of our group. In the Kingsboro church I came in contact with a group of star warriors, soldiers of light, who set me on the path to serve God fully. These youth, ranging from fifteen years of age to the early twenties, were on fire. It was evident that they were not your average Brooklyn kids. They were warriors with a mission and purpose. They conducted their own Bible studies, often poring through the books of Daniel and Revelation. They met weekly for prayer and fasting and were actively engaged in witnessing and outreach. In them, I saw Daniel 12:3 in action: "And they that be wise shall shine as the brightness of the firmament; and they that turn many to righteousness as the stars for ever and ever" (Daniel 12:3).

Every week the young people from this group shared stories of preaching in some church and how powerful it was. I didn't know that young people could be interested in anything other than the things of the world. Now I was seeing it firsthand. Their decided stance for the Word of God impressed me. I began to see them as stars of a different nature. My fame, at that time, was based on selfishness; I was famous in the eyes of this world. But these stars were famous in the eyes of an unseen world. They were "stars" because they were reflecting the light of the Sun of Righteousness, Jesus Christ. The sword of darkness I once wielded in the world was much different from the sword possessed by these youth—"the sword of the Spirit, which is the word of God" (Ephesians 6:17).

In the world I had a "crew." We drank together and partied together. We were ignorant warriors for the dark side. Now I was being introduced to a new "crew," one drawn together by the need for mutual protection and warfare of a different nature. They could drink of the Spirit together and celebrate the victory of Jesus Christ together. It was my privilege to have these star warriors of light as my new close and personal friends and examples.

One Sabbath afternoon, one of these young warriors approached me and asked if I would lead out in their next Bible study. The fire was contagious. I agreed without hesitation. The Lord was beginning to train me to use the saber of truth and light. My desire to be used by the Lord was growing day by day. Through the influence of these young star warriors, I would slowly come to the conclusion to leave the recording industry. Were it not for their example, I may have remained in the black hole.

Now here I was with my family in the country, severed from the dark side and connected to the light. In the quiet backwoods of Fredericksburg, Virginia, Sean and I began to study the use of this new sword, God's light saber—His Word—even more intensely. We still had many questions, and our love for Bible study was only getting deeper. In the solitude of the country we could study uninterrupted for hours. The more I studied, the more I desired to share what I was learning. We would often end in discussions (arguments) with our parents over the Bible. These discussions often sent me back to the Word of God to sharpen my understanding.

My father resisted us the most. He had a critical mind, and he would argue against the Bible. We couldn't talk about the Bible with him without it becoming an argument. Rough around the edges, we would pound out our arguments, and the harder we pounded, the more resistant my parents became.

One day, as my father and I sat watching a commercial break during the news hour, something happened that could not have had better timing. I had been telling my father about the possibility of a computer chip being placed in people's hands as a way of carrying their money. It might also be used as a form of identification and that all this may have something to do with what the Bible called "the mark of the beast." My father scoffed at the idea. Now as we both watched a commercial for a credit card, it ended with these words: "Who knows? Maybe one day, we'll carry our money *in* the palm of our hand." At that moment the screen showed a computer chip in a woman's palm—and then the screen went black. I silently looked up to heaven with a prayer on my lips; my father's eyes were still glued to the screen. I knew what he was thinking. I turned to look at him. Silence. He was still looking at the screen, but he was obviously not watching what was now showing. His eyebrows had curled, a look Dad gets when he is in deep thought.

"Dad?"

He finally let his eyes connect with mine. "Do you have anything I could read about the mark of the beast?" he said in a most solemn voice. I couldn't believe what I was hearing.

"Tons, Dad!" My father asked me to get him the entire set of little Amazing Facts books I had read. Three days later, my father had read through twenty mini-books on Bible doctrines, prophecy, and lifestyle.

"All that you were saying is true," he told me. "I can't believe that this was all in the Bible." My dad was dumbfounded. He began to ask me question after question about the Bible. One morning he called me into his office and asked me to sit down. I thought I was in trouble. "I had a dream last night," he said, "and I need you to explain it to me." I wasn't an interpreter of dreams, and I wondered what dream he could have had that was so important and that made him so serious. "In this dream," he went on, "I was in the air, and I heard the most beautiful music I have ever heard in my life. And then I kept hearing the words 'Holy, Holy, Holy.' Then I woke up."

"Dad," I said, in amazement, "do you know those words are in the Bible?" His eyebrows curled. Pulling the Book off the shelf, I read Isaiah 6:1–3:

> In the year that king Uzziah died I saw also the Lord sitting upon a throne, high and lifted up, and his train filled the temple. Above it stood the seraphims: each one had six wings; with twain he covered his face, and with twain he covered his feet, and with twain he did fly. And one cried unto another, and said, Holy, holy, holy, is the LORD of hosts: the whole earth is full of his glory.

Tears began to well up in Dad's eyes. For men in the Jamaican military, crying is a rare phenomenon. It was even more rare to see my father cry. My father, who had been a warrior of the dark side, was now feeling the force and power of the personal Spirit of God moving on his soul. He, too, was being drawn from years of service in the dark empire.

While Dad was beginning to be broken by the Word, Mom kept up her resistance. My father, Sean, and I were now praying for Mom. This was a miracle in itself. Mom had grown up in the Presbyterian Church of God. Though she had not attended church for years, she had recently begun going again. Every time we spoke about the Bible, she fervently declared that she would never be anything other than a Presbyterian. But when I'd ask Mom what Presbyterians believed, she didn't know.

Though Mom began attending church every Sunday—mainly because Sean and I had become Adventists—her lifestyle still belonged to the dark side. We had a large extended family of cousins, aunts, and uncles, and all of us would often get together to party, sometimes weekly! These gatherings were complete with reggae music, alcohol, and cigarettes. Once Sean and I escaped the black hole, our attendance at these parties slowly ended. But Mom and Dad continued to be involved. Mom especially loved the family gatherings and saw nothing wrong with the things that went with them. Our decision to follow Christ caused her to see clearly that if she were to follow, she would have to give up this lifestyle. Therefore, whatever Mom could do to limit our discussion of the Bible, she did. She did not welcome Bible topics.

One Sunday, Mom came home and asked me a question that had obviously been troubling her. "Are Presbyterians Catholics?" she asked.

"Why?" I inquired.

"Well," she began, "today in church the minister had us repeat the Apostles' Creed. I don't remember the whole thing, but there was one line that confused me. It said 'I believe in the holy Catholic church.' Are Presbyterians different from Catholics?"

"Mom," I explained, "Presbyterians are Protestants. Protestants are different from Catholics in that they believe in the Bible, and the Bible only, while Catholics believe that tradition is just as important as the Bible as a source of truth. Mom, do you believe in the Bible only? Or do you believe that tradition is just as important?"

My mom thought for a moment. "I'm not Catholic, so why would I go to a church that believes like they do? I think the Bible only is what we are supposed to follow, right?"

I nonchalantly, but quickly, agreed, trying not to show my excitement. "Mom, would you like for Sean and me to show you what the Bible says about following the Word of God only?"

"OK," she replied. From these studies my mother and father eventually began to attend the Adventist church with us. Within two years, they, too, were baptized, leaving behind the dark empire, its parties, alcohol, and lifestyle. God was indeed training us with the light saber of His Word.

The more I studied, the more comfortable I became with the Word of God. But when people began to encourage me to go into full-time ministry, I felt inadequate. I was hesitant because of my past. I thought it would not glorify God if someone like me became a minister.

While we were living in Brooklyn, an evangelist came to the church to hold a series of meetings; I was excited. I never had been to an evangelistic meeting before. Watching him preach night after night, and seeing people's understanding grow, was like fanning a flame within me. The burning desire even overpowered my fear of public speaking. Performing in front of half-drunk people had been no problem for me. But speaking to the minds of fully sober, serious-thinking people had terrified me from childhood.

Thinking I could never preach—and yet having the flame ignited within me—was unbearable. When an opportunity was given for testimonies, I stood up to speak. Before a packed church, I again held a microphone in my hand. It was the first time I had stood before a crowd since leaving the dark side. "I want to praise the Lord," I began with an unspeakable feeling of both joy and guilt, "for what He has done in my life. For years I was living in darkness and rebellion. I made it to what I thought was the top of the world. But God intervened."

"Amen," the people responded. But in my mind I was saying to them, *Don't say "Amen." That means the devil has won.*

I continued, "God brought me the truths of His Word and delivered me from darkness."

"Amen," the crowd responded again.

"But," I began to choke up, "the devil knew that this truth would affect me so much that I would want to preach God's truth, so he took me so deep into rebellion that it's impossible now for me to serve God as an evangelist." Tears began to flow freely from my eyes. "My past is too corrupt for God to use me in His vineyard. I would be a disgrace to His service. But I thank Jesus for saving me anyway."

It was my first time behind a microphone again. It was sweet yet bitter. I felt that a minister had to have a good past to serve in any capacity in the Lord's work. I did not have that clean past. Though I felt the burning desire to preach, I believed that God could not use me without disgracing His work.

After spilling my heart, I took my seat again. After the meeting ended that night, I expected to receive sympathy from those who understood my plight—that I couldn't be used of God as I would like to be. To my surprise and utter confusion, people came to me and continued to encourage me to go into the ministry. Hadn't they heard what I said? I kept thinking, *God can't be leading these people. Do they expect God to use junk for the sacred work of preaching the gospel?* I decided the people were wrong to encourage me to enter the ministry. *No*, I thought, *I will not speak publicly for Him no matter that His Word is like a fire within me.* I put away the thought.

Months later, as the conviction did not dwindle, but grew stronger, I sheepishly went to my pastor and told him that I felt the Lord was calling me into the ministry. He asked me one question: "Is there anything else you can see yourself doing?" I didn't have to think to answer that question. I could see myself doing nothing else. The pastor encouraged me to go to college so I could prepare to enter the ministry. Until this point, I had no idea that Seventh-day Adventists had colleges of their own.

In spite of the fire in my heart, doubts continued to settle around me because of my past. I put off a decision about the ministry. Unseen warriors of the dark side were once more fighting to regain my loyalty. By pressing on me a sense of unworthiness, they tried to keep me from God's calling for my life. As in the story of Joshua, the high priest who stood before God in the filthy garments of his past, Satan was at my right hand to accuse me before God of the filthiness of my past. Though I was active in church, I felt that I must not bring reproach on God.

Late in the summer of 1996 I was invited to a spiritual retreat. I happened to be sharing a cabin with the speaker of the event. After confessing to him that it wasn't possible for me to be a minister even though I felt the call, he simply said, "What doest thou here, Elijah?" This was the response God had given to Elijah when he hid from the wicked queen Jezebel. God had called Elijah for a purpose and for a mission. Elijah was to be a soldier of light, a star warrior. But here he was hiding in a cave! Now, God's words to Elijah were His words to me. "Why are you hiding in a cave when I have called you to serve Me? Why have you allowed your past to send you into hiding?"

I had never seen His plan for my life so clearly.

Suddenly there was a rushing mighty wind. Though I could not physically feel it, that wind blew away every excuse, every accusation, and every leaf of guilt that littered my soul. It was like a strange but refreshing storm, blowing away the doubt I had wrestled with. And yes, I rode the winds of this storm. God was calling me to be a star again, but this time for the kingdom of heaven. Again I heard that faint, inaudible whisper of the Spirit of God: *"I will bring you again before many."* The microphone I was now to use was to glorify God through the spoken word, the light saber of truth. God was calling me, as He had called so many others, to strike back against the dark empire!

Brothers forever: Sean and Ivor.

Ivor with his older brother, Rhoan.

16
A
NEW
CHAPTER

Day after day I eagerly waited. The mail carrier would pull up, open the black mailbox at the front of our property, and drive off. I would immediately head for the mailbox. The letter I was waiting for finally came. The return address on the envelope was from Oakwood College, a Seventh-day Adventist school located in Huntsville, Alabama. This was the big moment. I impatiently tore the letter open. "Dear Ivor, We are happy to inform you . . ." I began to jump for joy. I was accepted. I was going back to college to become a minister of the gospel! For the first time in my life I was looking forward to going to school and thoroughly studying my subjects. I was going to be a student among students!

The next few weeks I packed, shopped, organized my clothes, and did everything I could to prepare to go to the school of the prophets! I was looking forward to meeting new friends, to listening to the wisdom of seasoned teachers, to endless bliss in the school library! My parents were happy for me. I could sense the Lord's leading. This was a whole new chapter for me. Three years earlier, if someone had told me that I would be in school studying for the ministry, I would have laughed it off. But now it was reality.

Dad drove with me from Virginia to Huntsville. It was September 1997. The ten-hour trip seemed to pass in the blink of an eye. Before I knew it, we were driving through the entrance of Oakwood College.

The campus seemed divine, beautifully situated amid oak trees and lush lawns. That first week would be one of orientation for all new students. I had no friends, but I wasn't nervous, because everyone on campus was technically my brother or sister in Christ. I felt at home. I began meeting people the first day—Melvic, Andre, Aretha, Benjamin, John, Keetric, Chris, and many others. By the middle of orientation week, I was already leading out in impromptu Bible studies. Not that I had come to Oakwood to teach; no, I had come to learn. But that didn't quench my desire to share what the Lord had done for me. The very air of the campus seemed holy. It was a blessing to be around such a cloud of witnesses. Here I met many other soldiers of light, other young people who were on fire for God and who would have a deep impact on my life. It was amazing to see this movement—our church—embrace such an incredible diversity of nationalities and backgrounds. From the start, God was keeping the fire alive in my heart as I mingled with many people and became involved with Bible studies on campus.

A few weeks after my first semester, a fellow student approached me and asked if I would share my testimony at a student week of revival. I thought, *This soon, Lord?* I had never given my full testimony before an audience, and I was feeling nervous. But I accepted, knowing that this was God's will. When the Week of Prayer came, I was prayed up and prepared, yet still nervous. That night as I sat on the platform waiting to speak, I thanked God for allowing me the opportunity to share what He had done for me. I was still nervous, but I spoke for fifteen minutes to a captivated audience—captivated not by my words but by God's power to deliver from the black hole. After that night, I was fully convinced there was nothing else I could or would do but preach the wonderful message of salvation to a lost world.

Soon I was being asked to share more and more often on campus. Every opportunity thrilled my soul. Nothing was comparable to this experience. It infinitely surpassed the thrill I had received from worshiping audiences in the entertainment field!

Unlike my experience at Virginia State University, I had no physical conflicts with anyone at Oakwood College. I did have one close altercation. I was sitting in theology class one day when a young man and his brother who were seated in front of me became disruptive as the teacher spoke. I endured them as long as I could and then I said, "Shhhh!" The brothers turned and looked at me in a challenging way. I paid them no more attention. What would have turned into a fight in my previous life was over in a moment. I was more concerned with hearing the Word of God. I didn't see these two individuals in the class again. I decided they must be uninterested in theology and had dropped out.

A few months later, my good friend Benjamin invited a group of us to have lunch at his home. We got into a spiritual discussion. Two of the young men present, Jeremiah and his brother John, seemed interested in the discussion. Later, I asked if they'd be interested in learning how to study the Bible. They quickly accepted. We met regularly to study the Word and soon became good friends. In our first study, we took the shortest text in the Bible, John 11:35, which says, "Jesus wept." I told them to ask the text as many questions as they could think of and to write as much as they could in response to those questions. The next day they came back with three pages of thoughts on that one verse. One of these young men eventually changed his major to theology. One day we began trying to figure out where we had first met. Suddenly we realized that it hadn't been at Benjamin's house but in theology class! They were the two brothers with whom I had almost had the altercation! Today Jeremiah is a powerful preacher of the Word of God. God had taken my only potential enemies and made them two of my most precious friends. What a difference life made on the "light side"!

One night I was leaving one of the school buildings when I heard someone call out in a surprised voice, "Yoda!" I turned to see who had called me by my former stage name. I didn't recognize him, but he recognized me. He introduced himself as Myon. He was surprised to see me at Oakwood College as a student, and he proceeded to tell me how he had listened to my music. I shared with him briefly why I had left it. We became friends quickly. He introduced me to some other people on campus who were involved in "Christian" hip-hop. Over the course of the semester, I had frequent conversations with many of these individuals about why I left the entertainment industry.

I was interested to see what the women on campus were like. I watched and saw major differences between what I had been used to and what I now saw. It was incredible to see and hear young women talk about Jesus and their love for the gospel. This was strange to me, but I was moved by it.

One Sabbath, Myon invited me to attend church with him. We had spent much of the night before in a Bible study at his house. Myon was just beginning to make his way back to a full commitment to Christ. As we talked that night, we felt the Spirit of God moving. On Sabbath morning, when the pastor made the appeal, Myon was one of the first to walk down the aisle. When I saw him start forward, I walked down the aisle with him to encourage him. The woman I would someday marry, my princess, was in the audience that morning, but, of course, I didn't know it. She saw me walking down to the front with Myon and thought, *Who is that?*

After the service, Myon invited me to lunch at a friend's house. I hesitated, feeling funny about going to someone's home uninvited. But I had no other way to get back to my dorm room, so I went. A pretty, smiling young woman answered the door, surprised to see an uninvited guest—the person she had seen earlier walk down the aisle with Myon. When we were introduced, she could barely get my name right and didn't let go of my hand. "Ivir?" she questioned. "Evor? Evar? Oh! Ivor?" Little did I realize that this was my wife-to-be. Her name, I learned, was Atonte.

Although she had a house full of guests, Atonte and I talked the whole time. Myon began to tell her about my past. "Do you remember the group The Boogie Monsters?" he asked.

"No," she said, chuckling at the name.

After failing to jog her memory, Myon continued, "Ivor used to be a hip-hop artist, and now he's given it up. He's studying theology."

"Wow, you?" Atonte replied. Without letting me answer, Myon shot back, "Yes, I used to listen to them!"

"How would you like to be interviewed live on radio?" Atonte asked me. She was a cohost of a live call-in program on the college station WOCG. I could immediately see the passion of God in her soul. I would learn that it had not always been so.

Just before Atonte was born, her mother recommitted her life to Jesus. As a child, Atonte was spiritual, but as she got older, the dark side took hold of her. Like so many other young people, she joined the rebellion against the Prince of light. The dark side marked her high school and early college years. But one day while sitting on a rock at a Greek fraternity party at a college in San Francisco, Atonte heard the Spirit of God speaking to her in a still, small voice: *"What are you doing here?"* She then felt a distinct impression to go to Oakwood College. Just as angels of light had pierced the environment of marijuana with a message of salvation for me, they also pierced the dark party environment to reach Atonte. She was so moved by that impression that she jumped up from the rock and called her mother and told her she was ready to enroll at Oakwood. Her mother was excited because she had been begging Atonte to attend a Christian college.

When Atonte arrived at Oakwood College, she started doing the same things she had always done—parties, clubs, and drinking. The only difference was that she also attended weekly church services at the Oakwood College church where hundreds of young Christian college students were present. She was studying broadcast journalism and started working at the local college radio station. As she learned the trade of radio broadcasting, she was also beginning to listen to the messages that were being shared over the airwaves. She found herself recording some of the Christian music that she was playing and taking it home for her own use. Soon her life began to change. Her desire for the things of this world began to lose its power.

During her senior year Atonte found herself involved in a bad relationship. She desperately wanted out, but was controlled, as is often the case. One night while attending prayer meeting, Atonte knelt down and whispered a simple prayer to God, "By any means necessary, please save me from this relationship, Lord." A few days after that prayer was whispered she caught her boyfriend cheating on her. In spite of the hurt and pain, God gave her the strength to end the relationship.

While in college, Atonte worked hard to get as much hands-on experience as she could. She did several internships every summer. One internship was at NBC News in New York City. This gave her a real taste of the industry and what it was like to live in New York. A few days after she graduated from Oakwood College, she received a job offer in new production at CBS News in New York City. The offer was tempting, but Atonte was impressed by the Holy Spirit to turn it down. She did not want to live in the city. She decided to remain in Huntsville and continue to work at the Christian radio station. She had no idea what God had planned for her, but she felt total peace with her decision.

So here we were—Atonte and me—convinced our meeting was by divine appointment. Atonte had asked to interview me on radio. It would be my first time behind a studio microphone on the light side. Atonte's listening audience was the Oakwood campus. I thought, *This is it. This is how God is fulfilling my request for Him to put me behind a microphone again before many people.* In my mind I was ready to go back on the airwaves.

We continued talking. After a while, Atonte disappeared into the kitchen. Within moments a woman inconspicuously poked her head around the corner. Our eyes met, and she smiled. I would later find out that this was Atonte's mother who was checking me out at her daughter's request.

We began to call each other often. During the next few months, Atonte and I began doing hospital evangelism and door-to-door work together. She was one of the most spiritual young women I had met on campus. She was always excited about sharing her faith and took every opportunity to do so.

One semester later, my brother Sean enrolled at Oakwood College. From our childhood, we had done everything together. We played Batman and Robin together as children; we got involved in the martial arts and break dancing together as teenagers; we started our hip-hop group, were baptized as Baptists, got our record deal, converted to Adventism, were rebaptized, and left the music industry together—and now we were at Oakwood College together! Though our time at Oakwood would overlap only during one semester, God blessed us during our time there.

One day Sean came to me with a dream. In this dream he saw the lightning of God strike down and separate him and me. This was scary; the dream indicated separation, but we didn't know how it would happen. We would find out soon enough.

Atonte and I continued to do Bible work together; we took a canvassing team to my hometown in Virginia. The more time we spent together, the more I knew that she was the woman for me. Our relationship was so different from anything I had experienced before. Atonte was on fire for

God. She was beautiful and spiritual. There was no superficiality about her.

Our relationship continued to grow. We were able to share a lot with each other; our mutual love for spiritual things was a strong connection. She often tells me that had she met me with dreadlocks, she wouldn't have married me. She was intrigued with my past—not because I had been a star but because God had called me out of such darkness. We would often talk about my friends' decision to stay in the group. I shared with her my hopes that all of them would eventually see the light.

One evening the phone rang in my dorm room. I answered it.

"Hey," the voice on the other end responded.

"Mondo!" I shouted. I would know that voice anywhere.

"I'm out," he said quickly.

"What did you say?" I asked.

"I gave up my contract."

I couldn't believe my ears. "What happened?" I asked.

"God shut the label down to save me," he replied.

I couldn't believe what I was hearing. "Again? The label that picked you guys up folded?"

You'll recall that while Sean and I were still in the group, and just before we were to record our second album, Pendulum, a subsidiary of EMI records, shut down. All its groups, including ours, were picked up by another label. Now Mondo was telling me the label that had picked them up had shut down, as well! *What are the odds of that happening twice to one group?* I thought.

"When you and Sean left, a struggle was going on inside my heart," Mondo continued. "Eventually, I prayed and asked God that if this wasn't His will for me that He would provide a way out of the contract. The next thing I knew, our manager called us, saying, 'You guys won't believe this. I have bad news; the label is folding.' I knew this was God speaking. Vex wanted to shop for another label, but I told him I couldn't continue."

Mondo had escaped the black hole! Now he wanted to do ministry for the Lord, someway, somehow. I couldn't help remembering the dream Vex had had. *Three down, one to go!* I thought.

When I told Atonte about Mondo, she shared my joy. I saw the Lord working in mysterious ways. The cycle was being completed. At Christmas break 1997, Atonte went home to California. I went home to Virginia. We both had been invited to preach our first sermons at our home churches on December 21. That made us realize that God had called us to do ministry together on a permanent basis. With Atonte by my side, I felt ready to do whatever the Lord asked. With her, I would be complete. We were soon engaged to be married.

Even though I had given my life to Christ, there were times when I could feel the breath of the dragon's wrath. Atonte owned a 1990 BMW. One day I was driving her car. After a quick workout at the gym, I jumped into her car and threw my backpack in the backseat. I turned the key in the ignition and was backing out of the parking spot when I heard a loud pop. Flames shot out from beneath the hood. Then—BANG!—the front of the car exploded! *This is it! I'm about to die!* I thought. I managed to open the door and jump out of the car before a second explosion occurred and the whole car went up in flames. It was like something out of the movies! As I lay there on the ground, I remembered my backpack with my bible and other Bible-study materials in the backseat. I tried to run back to the car to get my books, but the flames were too hot. Someone called the fire department, but it seemed like an eternity before they got there. Once the firemen had put the fire out, I walked slowly toward the car, still in shock. The vehicle was totally consumed. I looked in the backseat, and there was my book bag—melted and drenched with water. I picked it up, took it over to a nearby lawn, and shook it. Out fell my Bible, Spirit of Prophecy books, and prophecy magazines, untouched by fire or water! I fell to my knees, awed by God's power and graciousness. Not only did He save my life, but He also saved my books! I could sense that this had been an effort by evil angels to take my life.

I thanked God, as well, that Atonte was more concerned about me than the BMW! We were married within a year. I had found my princess, a daughter of the God of heaven.

Atonte working at WOCG, the radio station where she first interviewed Ivor. Oakwood College, 1997.

Ivor and Atonte at Oakwood College.

17
STRIKING BACK AGAINST THE EMPIRE

Driving across the hot desert highway to Paso Robles, California, I wondered what lay ahead for us. I had come so far from darkness. My past seemed like another age. By my side was my bride and now partner in ministry. I had escaped from the black hole of the dark empire. I had started a new page in my history, but even that had taken an unexpected turn. I had planned to be at Oakwood for three years and graduate. But after Atonte I were married, I left school . . . again! This time it wasn't to pursue a record deal but to accept a position as a pastor. Atonte's home church, a small congregation of about thirty, was looking for a lay pastor. The congregation asked me if I would be willing to come and fill that position.

Imagine my parents' frustration; to them, I seemed to be as one tossed with the winds of a storm! Even I was beginning to wonder about my actions. But I felt that God was calling me to make this move. Since I had stepped out by faith from the black hole, I could see nothing of the future clearly. Every step was a step of faith, this one included. I had become a faith walker!

I plowed ahead. Sean and I had never been separated. Now I was headed to the West Coast, while he had left Oakwood to go to another school on the East Coast. He eventually became a pastor on the East Coast, while I was doing the same on the West Coast. This was the lightning that seperated. God would use us both as star warriors.

As a faith walker, I knew the gravitational pull of the black hole could have no power over me as long as I kept looking to Jesus. But most importantly, I knew that God had called me specifically to strike back against the empire that had once dominated me. Millions of souls were still trapped in this empire, and God wanted me to share my testimony about how I had escaped through His power. I was to be a star warrior of light. I was to ally myself with the forces of light, truth, and love.

I knew my mission. A black hole is really a massive star that "dies" or collapses into a dense object whose gravitational pull becomes so great that not even light can escape from it. A black hole may rightly be called a death star. The entertainment industry is just that, a death star, a black hole. And the goal of many of God's star warriors is to reveal and destroy this last-day death star that has set up its headquarters in the hearts of millions of young people. From the East Coast my brother would attack this massive death star, and I would do my part from the West Coast.

Leaving the future in God's hands, we made our way across the country to a small town in central California. I didn't know that most of the people in this little church were white. Afterward, I thought, *God is incredible. He's taken an ex–hip-hop, Jamaican born, New York City raised, one time black activist artist, to Paso Robles, California, to pastor a predominantly white flock!* There were two Seventh-day

Adventist churches in the area. Besides our little church, there was a sizable congregation of about two hundred or so members just three miles away in Templeton, California.

God blessed as I struggled through the lessons of leading a tiny flock. I would often ask the Lord, *How in the world are You going to use me here in the backwoods of Paso Robles, California, to strike back against the empire?*

We moved in with Atonte's parents until we could find our own home to rent. While in Paso Robles I was introduced to Three Angels Broadcasting Network (3ABN), an Adventist television network started in 1984 by the leading of God. Until then, I hadn't known it existed. As I watched the broadcasts, I was excited to see the different speakers, all sharing the truth of the three angels' messages.

We often went back to visit my parents in Virginia. My older brother Rhoan and his wife, Stacey, had now moved to Virginia. On one of our trips, Atonte and I got a chance to study the Bible with Rhoan, Stacey, and another married couple with whom they were friends. Earlier, I had tried to witness to my brother, but I turned him off with my hard spirit and debating attitude. Now, leading a flock was beginning to teach me lessons of tenderness. As I shared with them the words that I had often shared before, it was as though the Spirit of God was able to take them and do what I could not have done in my own strength. Rhoan and Stacey were eventually baptized into the church. It was an honor to have my older brother join us on the light side. I thought, *Three down, one to go!* My oldest brother, Tony, still living in Jamaica, had not yet given his life to Christ.

At my small church, I would often hold Friday night Bible studies, and some of the members from the neighboring

Templeton church began to attend. One of these was Dr. Stephen Mulder, an anesthesiologist. After hearing my story, Dr. Mulder decided to write an article about it for the Templeton church newsletter. The story was later submitted to the church's regional magazine, the *Pacific Union Recorder,* and was published. As a result, I began to get a few invitations to speak at different churches.

A Korean pastor read my testimony and invited me to speak to his Korean congregation. This engagement opened the door for me to minister to many Korean groups in California, including a two-week yearly training seminar for Korean youth. Here I had the privilege of striking against the dark empire by calling these young kids and teenagers out of the black hole. I saw many young people giving their lives fully to the Lord, being baptized, and picking up the torch of truth. And so I thought, *This must be it! The Lord led me to California to witness to these kids and get them to turn their lives around. This is my mission, the significance of the microphone in my hand in the dream.*

The Lord was beginning to bless our ministry. But we were now experiencing together the heat of the dragon, as well. We were living in an expensive area, and the pay of a lay pastor required me to work a second job. I took a job at Staples. During this time we experienced many ups and downs. Sometimes we had discouraging trials. Satan seemed to be in my face saying, "Look at your struggles! You had it made—money for life—and now look at you." Once I was so discouraged I was crying silently in the backyard. With closed eyes, I lifted my head heavenward toward the starry sky and spoke out loud, "Lord, if You have called me to the ministry, show me a shooting star—and I don't want to be out here all night!" I opened my tear-filled eyes looking for the star. It came within two seconds. I closed my eyes again and spoke, "Lord, that was too soon. My eyes were blurry, and I couldn't really tell if that was a shooting star. Give me a little time and then show me again." Again I opened my tear-filled eyes, cleared them, and began to look and count. A second shooting star streaked across the sky before I could count to ten! It was a defining moment for me. It was as though God was saying, "Don't worry. I am with you. I know the plans I have for you!"

That summer of 1999, I was invited to speak at the Central California Conference camp meeting at Soquel. I shared my testimony on Sabbath morning. When I agreed to speak, I didn't realize the attendance on Sabbath morning at the Soquel camp meeting was anywhere from four thousand to six thousand people! It was by far the largest audience I ever had addressed. Now I felt that this was it! I was seeing the prophecy fulfilled that God had given about the microphone, about being brought before many people. "Surely, this is the fulfillment," I said to myself. After I shared my testimony at Soquel camp meeting, I began to get more invitations to other churches in California. God was truly blessing our ministry.

But things were beginning to get really hard for us. Financially, we were unable to keep afloat. We started looking for other ministry opportunities. My wife ran across an ad in the *Pacific Union Recorder* for a position at a school for troubled youth. She spoke with the president, Mr. Blondel, Sr. He was a nice man but at the time had no positions available. In that conversation, Blondel encouraged us to attend a meeting called ASI (Adventist Lay Services), an organization of businessmen who financially supported various ministries. We decided to go and see what it was all about. The convention was to be held in Sacramento, California.

While there, we were surprised to see and meet so many of the people we had seen on 3ABN broadcasts. I also met the founder of American Cassette Ministries, Al Newhart. I was aware that his catalog carried tapes of powerful speakers such as Doug Batchelor, C. D. Brooks, and many others. I eagerly asked Al what it would take to have a message included in the catalog. He asked me to send him a tape of one of my messages. I wondered if the Lord could be opening the door to an even wider exposure of the message about the black hole.

That same day, as Atonte and I were in the cafeteria at the ASI meetings, we saw Danny Shelton, president of 3ABN. Again excitement came over me. We approached Danny and told him how much we appreciated the broadcasts. Then I began to share with him my testimony about coming out the hip-hop scene. Danny looked at me as though I were speaking Swahili. "Why don't you talk to Molly," he said. "She'll take your information."

I thought, *That didn't go so well. Did I say or do something wrong?* Danny didn't seemed interested that I used to be a rapper.

Feeling shot down, I went and found Molly at the 3ABN booth. I told her a little of my story. She took my information, and I left. When the ASI meetings were over, nothing spectacular had taken place for our ministry. We felt out of place, not having any formal ministry. We returned home thankful for the experience but wondering why we had gone.

18
ANOTHER
BLACK
HOLE

My stomach was in knots. The Paso Robles church had called a meeting. It was bad news for our family. The church was no longer able to support us. They cried; we cried. We wanted to stay; they didn't want us to go.

We began immediately looking for any way to stay in ministry. We even went to the Korean community to see if there were any openings for a lay pastor. Without a college degree, I didn't stand much of a chance of getting hired by a conference. To our delight, three Korean churches wanted us—one in Sacramento, California, one in Napa Valley, California, and one in Oregon. We chose Napa Valley. We were again on a new mission.

The members of the larger neighboring church in Templeton held a going-away party for us. We had given notice to our landlord, had found a place to live in Napa Valley suitable for us and the two children we had by this time, and were all set to move—when we got the phone call. An elder of the church in Napa Valley was calling to tell us that things had not developed as planned, and the church would not be able to hire us after all. We were crushed. We had nothing.

I felt that I had entered another black hole. I knew that it was only by a miracle that I had been able to find a lay pastor position in the first place. Now it was over. *What are the odds of a door like this ever opening again?* I thought. I felt as if I had been cast out from God.

After a few days of intensive searching, we found a job opening for Atonte and myself at a radio station in Mississippi. *Mississippi?* I thought. *A black hole!* I did *not* want to live in Mississippi. There, I would be doing "technical work" (I didn't have the slightest idea what that meant), and my wife would be doing voice work. Our pay was minimal in exchange for free rent. Discouraged but with no other options, we said Goodbye to the ministry as we headed off to Magee, Mississippi.

We stopped first in Virginia to see my parents, stayed with them for a while, and then continued our journey. It was late at night when we arrived in Magee. We pulled up to the house. It was small. Atonte got out of the car with our children, Jaden and Joshua. I was the last one to enter the house. When I did, I began to cry. The condition of the house was deplorable, and a sense of failure flooded over me.

Eventually, we got ourselves under control. We would make the best of it. But in the coming days, I often struggled, wondering if this was the end of my call to the gospel ministry. Often I could feel Satan taunting me, "You gave up everything for *this?* Look at you now!" I would think about God's promise about the microphone, about His invitation to join the light side and become an active star warrior for Him. Things just didn't seem to add up. What in the world was I doing working as a technician at a radio station? It seemed that darkness had surrounded me and my future. God seemed silent, dismally silent.

One day as I sat in discouragement, the phone rang. The person on the other end of the line introduced herself as Miriam Newhart. I didn't recognize the name. She continued, "A few years ago you gave my husband, Al, a tape of one of your sermons. We just found the tape, listened to it, and want to know if you would be willing to do a recording of your testimony for our catalog." I was taken off guard. I had sent Al a tape of the message shortly after the ASI meeting, but I had never heard from him. I thought he had probably listened to it and then put the tape in the garbage or something.

Now Mrs. Newhart was asking if they could include my message in their catalog of tapes. "Of course," I replied. For the first time, my testimony was to go around the world. *Now,* I thought, *this is definitely it! The microphone in hand, the bringing before many people. . . . This is it. This is the fulfillment.* It seemed that God had saved this event for one of my most rainy days. And even while we were there in Mississippi, the Lord began to open opportunities for me to speak. We met many wonderful people in the churches.

We also had been keeping in touch with our friends back in California. One day I got a phone call from a member of the church in Templeton. The Templeton church had just lost its pastor to another area and had been without a pastor for some months. "Guess who our new pastor is going to be?" our friend asked. Before I could answer, she replied, "Steve Wohlberg!"

I had seen Steve on 3ABN and had read some of his books. "Steve?" I replied. I began thinking, *Why couldn't I have been around for this? I would have loved to have a mentor like Steve!*

Within two weeks of that conversation, our jobs in Mississippi were terminated. But just about the same time, a couple from our church back in Paso Robles made us a gracious offer. They would provide my salary to return to the church for ten months. After that, it would be a walk of faith. They could not have known how much this meant to us. We gladly packed our bags to head back to California. Atonte was six months pregnant with our daughter, Jenesis. On the trip to California, cheers went up every time we crossed a state line! We were excited to be coming back home and coming back to ministry. As I saw it, I just had escaped another black hole!

Ivor and Atonte are married. 1998.

19

"I WILL BRING YOU AGAIN"

We were back home in our tiny, but familiar, church in Paso Robles, California. Our reception was warm. Even the members of the Templeton Hills Seventh-day Adventist Church were happy to see us again. We had formed many friendships in both churches. Camp meeting was coming up in a few days, and for some reason, the Templeton members were eagerly anticipating my meeting Pastor Wohlberg.

When Steve and I were introduced, we hit it off immediately. And then one of the members from Templeton made a suggestion. "Wouldn't it be great if Ivor became our youth pastor?"

That could never happen, I thought. The Templeton Hills Church was full of professionals—and all Caucasians. Not that I had a problem with either professionals or Caucasians! I just thought, *How is God going to take an ex–hip-hop Jamaican, raised in New York, ex-pro black, dreadlocks wearing, activist, and make him the youth pastor in Templeton, California, in an all white, upper income church?* Within a month, the Templeton Hills Church had voted to bring me on as a part-time youth lay pastor. Within the year the two churches—Templeton Hills and Paso Robles—merged, and I was hired full time. Pastor Wohlberg traveled often and split pulpit duties with me fifty-fifty!

Steve also had a vision of having a radio program through LifeTalk Radio, based in Tennessee. He asked Atonte and me to be cohosts with him. It would be a live, nationally syndicated call-in program called *World News and the Bible.* I remember thinking to myself, *OK, this is really it. This is what God meant by the vision of the microphone in hand, the bringing again before many.*

While ministering as a lay youth pastor and also cohosting *World News and the Bible,* I also had the opportunity to re-sume speaking all around California. One weekend I went to speak at a Hispanic church. Atonte and I were staying with friends who were members of the church. After the meetings, Maria began to tell us that she wanted to record some cook-ing shows for 3ABN Latino. We thought that was an excel-lent idea and said we'd help her anyway we could. She was ready for help that weekend. Out came the camcorder. Atonte would be her mock cohost, and I would be the cameraman!

Maria sent in the recording hoping to get a response from 3ABN. After about six months, 3ABN contacted her and told her that they would like her to host her own cooking program for 3ABN Latino. She was excited, and we were happy for her. "I'm going to tell them about you, Ivor," she said.

"Maria, I spoke to 3ABN years ago," I told her. "Nothing happened then, and nothing probably will happen if you men-tion it." Undaunted, she insisted that she would anyway.

We continued growing in our ministry and watched the Lord bless in many ways. Early one morning, after we had fin-ished family worship, the phone rang. The caller ID read "Three Angels Broadcasting." "Atonte!" I yelled.

Terrified by my shout, she came running. "What is it?"

"It's 3ABN!" I couldn't even pick up the phone. Atonte answered as I listened. "Yes. Yes. Sure. September?" Still in disbelief, I waited for the short phone call to end.

"What did they say?" I demanded.

"They want you to give your testimony on *3ABN Today.*"

I couldn't believe it. *This is it. One shot, to blast the black hole, the death star. Millions of viewers, many hooked by the force. . . . This is it. "I will bring you before many"!*

Immediately another thought came to mind. I had watched *3ABN Today* many times. I knew different people did the interviews. I remembered my first encounter with Danny Shelton, 3ABN president, and how he hadn't seemed interested about my being a hip-hop artist. I began to pray, "Please, Lord, don't let Danny interview me. He'll probably be bored with me. He'll probably remember me from ASI. Let it be someone else—anyone else!"

When September came, our whole family flew out to 3ABN. Atonte was pregnant again with little Jaliyah. As I thought about the upcoming interview, I prayed the Lord would help me to say the right things. My greatest fear reared its head—not the fear of speaking in front of people but the fear of not saying the right thing.

The morning the program was to be recorded, I asked who would be doing the interviewing. We were told that Danny was a little under the weather, but he was planning to do the interview anyway. *Please, let it be somebody else,* I kept thinking. *Danny will probably be bored with what I have to say.*

A few minutes later, Danny walked in. *Oh boy, this is it; he is going to be bored with this interview.* But as soon as Danny said Hello to us, my spirit changed. *Maybe he might have some interest in this after all.* The interview proceeded and went well. During the interview I discovered why Danny had looked so puzzled back at the ASI meeting several years earlier when I first had spoken to him. He never had heard of hip-hop; he didn't know what it was! Then something else happened that allowed me to understand Gods's guiding in my life. Right in the middle of the program, Danny publicly invited us back to record a series of programs on 3ABN. Now here is a little secret to be kept just between you and me. When Danny publicly invited us to do these programs, I wanted to jump—jump like our group had done so long ago when we had cut a deal with the dark side to produce eight albums. I wanted to jump because God was bringing me again before many people to strike back against the dark empire. I wanted to jump because God's Word was being fulfilled in my life. I wanted to jump, but, instead, I kept peaceful. "We'd love to do that, Danny," I calmly replied.

Today, our ministry through 3ABN is taking us around the globe. Our program *Battles of Faith* has combined with other 3ABN programs to combat the forces of darkness. I thank God as I look back to see how He delivered me out of the black hole. I thank Him that "Yoda" and "Jedi"—myself and Sean—once warriors of darkness, are now both new creatures in Christ. I thank God that Sean and I are now pastors.

Shortly after our first 3ABN visit, Pastor Wohlberg left Templeton Hills to take up another ministry position in California. The church made the unusual move of requesting that I become its official pastor. In December 2005, the conference hired me to be the pastor of the Templeton Hills Seventh-day Adventist Church. The impossible became a reality. God had indeed brought me again!

20

WAR
OF THE
HILLS

Obviously, Satan is in an all-out war to secure the human race in the clutches of the dark empire. Through spiritualism, he is leading many souls astray. The black hole of Hollywood (the entertainment industry), the capital and black hole of the dark empire, is the primary medium through which this is being accomplished. The home of the stars means more than we think. Demonic star warriors (fallen angels) also have made this place, Hollywood, one of their headquarters. The war being waged through the entertainment industry is sucking many into its black hole.

There is something mystical and magical about Hollywood. Consider the name itself. Holly (*Ilex aquifolium*) is a tree that was used by the druids of the ancient stellar cult as a symbol of good will, peace, and happiness. They used it to ward off evil spirits and protect themselves. Druids—the name means "man with the wisdom of the wood"—utilized different wood, including the holly wood, to make magical wands. The tradition of sending boughs of holly accompanied by other gifts during Saturnalia, the Roman festival of Saturn that was held around the end of December, was popular with the ancient Romans. The holly tree, also known as the "holy" tree in some parts of Europe, was considered by the ancient druids to be the king of all trees, the holly king, or king of the forest. It was viewed as being powerful in warding off spirits and sorcerers and to communicate with elves and fairies.

For these reasons, the holly tree is one of nine sacred or holy trees in Wicca—a contemporary term for witchcraft. It is eye opening to note that the fictional character Harry Potter has a magic wand made of holly wood! Similarly, could *Hollywood* itself be a deadly magical wand in the hand of the master sorcerer, Satan?

The holly tree was used to cast spells of sleep and rest or to make the passage to death easier. It is no surprise, then, that through Hollywood the world has become more tolerant of spiritualism and sin. It is as though many are being lulled to sleep about the dangers behind "the seen." The red berries of the holly tree look inviting but are deadly to humans. So, the bright lights of the entertainment industry look inviting but are also deadly.

When we put all of this together, we see a hill, the Hollywood hill. We also see those words firmly planted in the ground, the symbol of the sacred holly tree and the entertainment industry. Hollywood invites us into a world of security, fame, riches, and, most of all, seemingly harmless fun. It is a hill where people are symbolically drawn to pay homage to the stars, to study them and learn to be like them. Yet, it is an entrance to the dark side.

But there is another hill. This hill, the place where Jesus was crucified, is called Calvary or Golgotha (see Matthew 27:33; Luke 23:33). Jesus once said, "And I, if I be lifted up from the earth, will draw all men unto me" (John 12:32).

His sacrifice for us on that hill draws us to Him in love. Hollywood is a magic wand in the hand of Satan, to draw people's minds to his holly hill and away from Christ's holy hill!

What is it the enemy does not want us to see about Calvary or Golgotha? When Adam and Eve sinned, they were promised a Deliverer who would break the spell of the enemy over their minds. In Genesis 3:15 the promise was stated thus: "And I will put enmity between thee and the woman, and between thy seed and her seed; it shall bruise thy head, and thou shalt bruise his heel." Jesus, the Messiah, the Morning Star, would bruise the head of the serpent, the fallen star, while the serpent would bruise His heel. This was fulfilled at Calvary. It was here that Jesus was bruised for our sins (see Isaiah 53:5). But Christ bruised the head of the serpent. How so? The word *Calvary* is the Greek word *kranion* from which we get our word *cranium* or *skull.* The Scripture says, "And when they were come unto a place called Golgotha, . . . a place of a skull . . . they crucified him" (Matthew 27:33, 35). When that *wooden cross* on which Christ was nailed went down into that skull-shaped hill, called Calvary and Golgotha, it symbolized the death blow to the head of the serpent. The moment Jesus died, there was a great earthquake; the skull was broken (see Matthew 27:50, 51). The death of Christ for sinners like you and me blew Satan's mind! Moreover, the Bible says that this event opened the graves of some of the righteous dead, those who were held bondage to death (see verses 52, 53).

So, when you and I focus on the hill of Calvary, on the tree with its bleeding Victim, something happens to our hard carnal minds. Our hard, rocky minds and hearts are broken because of His sacrifice. The sorcerer's power over us is broken.

Thus, we turn from the black hole, the holly hill, and are drawn instead toward Christ's holy hill. If we would escape from the black hole, we must turn our eyes on Jesus.

The hill in Hollywood seeks to blow our minds with the spectacular, the exciting, with false star wars, a false war of the worlds, and more. It hopes to draw us away from the hill of Calvary. But the gospel, rightly understood, will also blow our minds. There is a real star war going on, more mind-blowing than anything Hollywood can produce. If we could only open our eyes, the spell would be broken! The tree of Hollywood wants to draw us away from the tree of Calvary. Many, even professed Christians, are kneeling at the foot of the holly tree instead of at the foot of the tree at Calvary. The sacrifice at the hill of Calvary was of one Man that extends to millions the hope of eternal life. The sacrifice at the hill of Hollywood leads millions to lose their souls in eternal death.

I thank God for the many other star warriors I see escaping the black hole and telling their story. I thank God for repeating His power in the lives of many, many people today. And I thank God that He is not yet finished with my friends who went back. I often think about all my friends. Friends with whom I came into this truth, friends I studied with and was baptized with. God still has a purpose for them. He has revealed the truth to them, and I think of what might have occurred for God's glory if they had remained steadfast. But God is not finished with them yet. The verdict is not in. Though they are still trapped in the black hole, I know that God continues to call them.

The dark empire has many slaves, and through the death star (the entertainment industry) more are being captivated daily. Yet, God has called for star warriors from all over this world to strike back against the empire. By using the light saber of God's Word, star warriors may destroy the death star that reigns in the hearts of millions.

And there are many people whom I do not know who have escaped the dark hole through my testimony and the testimonies of others. There will be an exodus in the last days, a great prophetic movement away from the ways of this world, an exodus from Babylon, an exodus from the black hole. It is best summed up in the words of Revelation 18:

> And after these things I saw another angel come down from heaven, having great power; and the earth was lightened with his glory. And he cried mightily with a strong voice, saying, Babylon the great is fallen, is fallen, and is become the habitation of devils, and the hold of every foul spirit, and a cage of every unclean and hateful bird. For all nations have drunk of the wine of the wrath of her fornication, and the kings of the earth have committed fornication with her, and the merchants of the earth are waxed rich through the abundance of her delicacies.
>
> And I heard another voice from heaven saying, Come out of her, my people, that ye be not partakers of her sins, and that ye receive not of her plagues (verses 1–4).

At which hill will you worship? On which hill will you take your final stand? Which destiny do you want? Which star will you look to? May God guide this great exodus from the darkness of this world. May those trapped in the darkness of the black hole look up and see the light and follow it. May God's stars come out and shine!

Atonte and Ivor on the set of 3ABN television
with Danny Shelton, 3ABN president.
February 4, 2005.

Jaliyah, Atonte, Joshua, Ivor, Jaden, and Jenesis
Myers. 2006.

APPEAL

Imagine this . . .

An invitation has been sent out through the Cross of Calvary. It is an invitation to become part of a prophecy. The Bible foretells of a people who will hear the invitation and forsake the kingdom of darkness. It foretells of an innumerable company of warriors who having once served the prince of this world will become a mighty force against the powers of darkness. They will be heroes in a world shaken by an alien foe. They will, through honor, sacrifice, and the heroic death of their hero Jesus Christ, bring down the empire of evil. Having escaped the black hole of vice and destruction, they will lead others out of the same. The invitation has been extended to all.

This is no imaginary invitation and no imaginary battle. Will you accept the call?

More inspiring books from Pacific Press!

Grounds for Belief
Ed Dickerson

Change is inevitable—except from vending machines. Times change. It's not your daddy's world anymore. Today we live in a media-dominated, postmodern world. Facts and opinions bombard us via e-mail, cell phones, I-pods, and satellite TV. We're more connected electronically than ever before, but more of us feel isolated and lacking in close friends.

Is there such a thing as truth anymore? Ed Dickerson thinks so. He specializes in making Christianity accessible to contemporary audiences. Seekers, debaters, the proud, and the humble come to his Grounds for Belief cafe. Some come for the baked goods and others for games. Some come to condemn and some to praise, but all are welcome there. You, too. Come along and eavesdrop on the conversations.
Paperback, 144 pages   0-8163-2184-1   US$12.99

From Hollywood to Heaven
Steve Wohlberg

This is the gripping true story of Steve Wohlberg, well-known author and speaker. By his teenage years, "Tinseltown" had drawn Steve into a world of alcohol, drugs, and wild living. He could have ended up in prison—or worse, dead. But Steve was the object of a heavenly rescue mission.
Paperback, 144 pages   0-8163-2145-0   US$11.99

Demons in Disguise
Steve Wohlberg

Everyone knows death is real. But an increasing number of people are convinced there is a happy existence just beyond death's door, because they've seen a ghost. This notion is reinforced by movies and television programs. This book reveals bona fide examples of real spirits making contact with real people. An unseen world does exist. But the Bible warns us against being deceived. Not all of these entities are friendly.
Paperback   978-07684-2491-1   US$15.99

Order from your ABC by calling **1-800-765-6955**, or get online and shop our virtual store at **http//www.AdventistBookCenter.com**.
• Read a chapter from your favorite book
• Order online
• Sign up for e-mail notices on new products

Prices subject to change without notice.